THE ILLUSTRATED GUIDE TO
MODERN NAVAL AIRCRAFT

THE ILLUSTRATED GUIDE TO
MODERN NAVAL AIRCRAFT

Features a directory of 55 aircraft with 330 identification photographs

A history of shipborne fighters, bombers and helicopters, including the
Sea Vixen, A-6 Intruder, F-14 Tomcat, Sea Harrier, Merlin, and many more

FRANCIS CROSBY

southwater

This edition is published by Southwater

an imprint of Anness Publishing Ltd

Blaby Road, Wigston

Leicestershire LE18 4SE

info@anness.com

www.southwaterbooks.com

www.annesspublishing.com

Anness Publishing has a new picture agency outlet for images for publishing, promotions

or advertising. Please visit our website www.practicalpictures.com for more information.

Publisher: Joanna Lorenz

Senior Editor: Felicity Forster

Copy Editor: Will Fowler

Cover Design: Nigel Partridge

Designer: Design Principals

Production Controller: Bessie Bai

ETHICAL TRADING POLICY

At Anness Publishing we believe that business should be conducted in an ethical and ecologically sustainable way,

with respect for the environment and a proper regard to the replacement of the natural resources we employ.

As a publisher, we use a lot of wood pulp in high-quality paper for printing, and that wood commonly comes from spruce trees.

We are therefore currently growing more than 750,000 trees in three Scottish forest plantations: Berrymoss

(130 hectares/320 acres), West Touxhill (125 hectares/305 acres) and Deveron Forest (75 hectares/185 acres). The forests

we manage contain more than 3.5 times the number of trees employed each year in making paper for the books we manufacture.

Because of this ongoing ecological investment programme, you, as our customer, can have the pleasure and

reassurance of knowing that a tree is being cultivated on your behalf to naturally replace

the materials used to make the book you are holding.

Our forestry programme is run in accordance with the UK Woodland Assurance Scheme (UKWAS)

and will be certified by the internationally recognized Forest Stewardship Council (FSC).

The FSC is a non-government organization dedicated to promoting responsible management

of the world's forests. Certification ensures forests are managed in an environmentally sustainable

and socially responsible way. For further information about this scheme, go to www.annesspublishing.com/trees.

A CIP catalogue record for this book

is available from the British Library.

Previously published as part of a larger volume,

The World Encyclopedia of Naval Aircraft

NOTES: The nationality of each aircraft is identified in the specification box by the

national flag that was in use at the time of the aircraft's commissioning and service.

Although the information in this book is believed to be accurate and true at the time of

going to press, neither the authors nor the publisher can accept any legal responsibility

or liability for any errors or omissions that may have been made nor for any inaccuracies.

PAGE 1: **F-4 Phantom.** PAGE 2: **Sikorsky SH-60 Seahawk.** PAGE 3: **Sukhoi Su-33.** PAGE 5: **Dassault Rafale.**

Contents

6 Introduction

A HISTORY OF MODERN NAVAL AIRCRAFT

10 Naval air power and the
Korean War
12 US Navy carriers and the
Vietnam War
14 Naval aircraft armament since 1945
16 Aircraft carriers of the
Falklands War
18 Naval aviation technology –
1945 to the present day
20 Target – Libya
22 A 21st-century carrier at war
24 Current and future carriers
26 Top Gun

AN A–Z OF MODERN NAVAL AIRCRAFT

30 Agusta Westland EH 101 Merlin
32 Armstrong Whitworth (Hawker)
Sea Hawk
34 BAE SYSTEMS Harrier/
Sea Harrier
36 Beriev A-40/Be-42 Albatross
38 Beriev Be-12
40 Blackburn Buccaneer

42 Boeing/McDonnell Douglas/
Northrop F/A-18 Hornet
44 Boeing/McDonnell Douglas/
Northrop F/A-18E Super Hornet
46 Breguet Alizé
48 Dassault Etendard and
Super Etendard
50 Dassault Rafale
52 de Havilland Sea Venom
54 de Havilland Sea Vixen
56 Douglas Skyraider
58 Douglas F4D Skyray
60 Douglas A-3 Skywarrior
62 Fairey Gannet
64 Grumman A-6 Intruder
66 Grumman F9F-2 Panther
68 Grumman F9F Cougar
70 Grumman F-14 Tomcat
72 Grumman F11F Tiger
74 Grumman F7F Tigercat
75 Grumman Tracker
76 Grumman/Northrop Grumman
E-2 Hawkeye
78 Hawker Sea Fury
80 Kaman SH-2 Seasprite
81 Kamov Ka-25
81 Kamov Ka-27
82 Lockheed S-3 Viking
84 Lockheed Martin F-35
Lightning II

86 Martin P5M Marlin
87 McDonnell F2H Banshee
87 McDonnell F3H Demon
88 McDonnell Douglas A-4 Skyhawk
90 McDonnell Douglas F-4 Phantom II
92 Mikoyan-Gurevich MiG-29K
94 North American FJ Fury
96 North American A3J/A-5 Vigilante
98 ShinMaywa PS-1/US-1
100 Sikorsky S-51/Westland Dragonfly
102 Sikorsky SH-60 Seahawk
104 Sikorsky CH-53E Sea Stallion and
MH-53 family
106 Sukhoi Su-33
108 Supermarine Attacker
109 Supermarine Scimitar
110 Vought A-7 Corsair II
112 Vought F-8 Crusader
114 Westland Lynx
116 Westland (Sikorsky) Sea King
118 Westland Wasp
120 Westland Wessex
122 Westland (Sikorsky) Whirlwind
123 Westland Wyvern
124 Yakovlev Yak-38

126 Glossary
126 Key to flags
127 Index
128 Acknowledgements

Introduction

The first time an aircraft was launched from a ship was in 1910, when pilot Eugene Ely took off from the USS *Birmingham* and landed nearby after just five minutes in the air. From this first daring, experimental flight was born one of the most potent manifestations of military might – naval air power.

The design and development of naval combat aircraft has always been challenging. In the early days of military aviation, naval aircraft were created simply by modifying existing landplanes and rendering them suitable for the harsh environment of carrier operations. Unfortunately, the addition of essential equipment such as arrestor hooks and beefed-up undercarriages, as well as strengthened structures, frequently eroded the performance edge an aircraft may have enjoyed as a landplane. This led to a built-in inferiority compared to land-based types. Only when naval aviation proved its strategic value in World War II did purpose-designed, high-performance combat aircraft start to appear – aircraft that could hold their own over water or land. As a result, naval aviation became a war-winning factor.

Nations such as the United States are still able to project their military power anywhere they can sail their carriers. These vast ships, some as complex as cities, enable military

TOP: **A Royal Navy carrier showing what were, in their day, the most advanced aircraft in the Fleet Air Arm inventory – Sea Hawks and Sea Venoms.**
ABOVE: **The decade after the end of World War II saw many advances in aerodynamics. The Grumman F11F was the Second US Navy aircraft to break the sound barrier.**

planners to field some of the world's most potent aircraft types and, if required, launch strikes against potential enemies around the world without the need for land bases.

Carriers are free to roam the seas, which make up 70 per cent of the Earth's surface, while not entering other countries' national waters. Aircraft carriers' speed and flexibility enable them to bring firepower in the form of naval air power anywhere in the world in a matter of days.

ABOVE: **The Merlin, a joint venture between Italy and Britain, is one of the most capable helicopters in military service today. The aircraft's two computers manage its mission system and the aircraft is controlled by a hi-tech glass cockpit. The helicopter is now a vital element of naval air power.**
LEFT: **The unique Harrier/Sea Harrier family of fighter and attack aircraft gave naval strategists the vertical take-off capability of helicopters but with the high performance of jet fighters. The type first saw action flying from ships during the Falklands War in 1982.** BELOW: **The flying boat, with its ability to patrol vast areas of ocean, had its heyday in World War II, but some new flying boats were introduced post-war, including the Martin P5M Marlin.**

This book brings together information and data about naval aircraft from the immediate post-World War II period to the present, and indeed the next generation of naval combat aircraft such as the Lockheed Martin F-35. It is interesting to note that with some types of versatile, modern combat aircraft, including the F-35 and the Rafale, naval versions are planned from the outset in parallel with land-based versions.

The reader will also find information about the early naval jet aircraft, flying boats and helicopters. One of the most significant developments in post-war naval air power has been the increasingly important role played by helicopters. Novelty flying machines then flying ambulances, choppers were soon developed into rotary aircraft capable of carrying nuclear weapons.

The author had to make difficult choices, and the A–Z listing does not claim to feature every post-war naval aircraft ever built. It does, however, present the individual stories of the aircraft that the author believes to have been the most significant. The specifications are presented in a standard form to enable the reader to make comparisons of power, armament, size, weights and performance.

The performance figures quoted are to give a broad indication of an aircraft's capabilities, which can vary considerably even within the same marks of a type. The carriage of torpedoes and drop tanks can affect performance – even radio aerials can reduce top speed. The performance should be seen as representative and not definitive.

A History of Modern Naval Aircraft

Combat aircraft have played an increasingly important role in conflict since they came into their own during the pioneering days of air warfare in World War I. Naval aviation, that is military aviation that takes place from fighting ships, was born in 1911 when a Curtiss biplane landed on a wooden platform built on the cruiser USS *Pennsylvania* and took off from it again. Although seen by most more as a stunt than a demonstration of the potential of naval air power, it proved the concept. The first true carrier with an unobstructed flight deck did not enter service with the Royal Navy until the last stages of World War I, but by the end of World War II the carrier was seen to be a mighty warship with the potential to project a nation's power more flexibly than the large battleships that once ruled the waves.

The importance of carriers today is best demonstrated by former US President Bill Clinton, who said, "When word of crisis breaks out in Washington, the first question that comes to everyone's lips is: 'Where is the nearest carrier?'" Nuclear-powered and nuclear-armed supercarriers were the ultimate development. These small floating cities are a far cry from the converted ships from the pioneering days of aircraft operating from naval craft.

LEFT: **The French Dassault Rafale M, pictured here with a US Navy carrier, was designed from the outset as a naval variant of a new high-performance combat aircraft. As budgets get tighter, aircraft designed solely for naval operations will become rarer.**

Naval air power and the Korean War

Shortly after World War II ended, the US Navy's plans for the next generation of 'supercarriers' were sidelined due to the influence of the US Air Force who at that time, with Strategic Air Command, dominated US military thinking. The Korean War, however, reinforced the value of carriers and the need for a larger, more capable 'supercarrier'.

The United Nations began carrier operations against North Korean forces on July 3, 1950, in response to the invasion of South Korea. UN Task Force 77 at that time consisted of the US Navy carrier USS *Valley Forge* and Britain's HMS *Triumph*. Although the UN had air supremacy, having effectively neutralized the threat posed by the North Korean Air Force, the North Korean ground forces virtually overran South Korea – only a small area in the south-east near the port of Pusan held out.

By mid-September 1950, three US Navy Essex-class aircraft carriers were available for Korean War operations: in addition to *Valley Forge, Philippine Sea* and *Boxer* were on station. *Valley Forge* and *Philippine Sea* each carried two squadrons of F9F Panther jet fighter-bombers and two of propeller-driven World War II-vintage F4U Corsair fighter-bombers as well as a squadron of Skyraider attack aircraft. *Boxer* had an all-propeller air group that comprised four squadrons of Corsairs and one of Skyraiders. Britain's HMS *Triumph* fielded two squadrons of Fireflies and Seafires. The US escort carriers *Badoeng Strait* and *Sicily* each also provided a base for US Marine Corps' F4Us, which were specialists in close-air support for ground forces.

On September 15, the UN made an amphibious landing at Inchon, some 160km/100 miles up the west coast from Pusan, as the UN forces at Pusan counter-attacked. The Inchon landing succeeded only because of the air support available from the UN's carriers, and by the end of September virtually all organized North Korean forces had been subdued or driven north of the 38th parallel.

TOP: **USS *Lake Champlain*. Fire was a major hazard on carriers and required prompt action to stop its spreading. Unignited fuel pouring from an aircraft jet pipe posed a major threat and any fire could prove deadly.** ABOVE: **The Vought Corsair, often thought of as only a World War II combat aircraft, was a key aircraft in the United States' Korean War inventory. In the first year of the war, the Corsair flew 80 per cent of all US Navy and US Marines close-support missions. Night-fighter versions were deployed and in a pure fighter role the Corsair tangled with and destroyed enemy jets.**

As the war progressed, the carriers continued to support UN ground troops together with land-based UN aircraft that could now operate from recaptured airfields. By early November 1950, UN troops were facing increasing numbers of Chinese troops who were now openly supporting North Korea. UN forces attempted to arrest the Chinese advance by destroying the crossings of the Yalu river. Between November 9 and 21, aircraft of a now greatly enlarged Task Force 77 – Skyraiders and Corsairs escorted by Panthers – flew 593 sorties against the road and rail bridges across the Yalu. On November 9 an F9F Panther flying from the USS *Philippine Sea* became the first US Navy jet to achieve an aerial victory in combat when it shot down a MiG-15 during a raid on a Yalu target.

In May 1951, United States Navy Skyraiders carried out the only aerial torpedo attack of the Korean War, but not against a maritime target. Despite attacks by ground troops and B-29 bombers against the strategically important Hwachon dam, the structure had remained intact. But on May 1, eight Douglas AD-1 Skyraiders from USS *Princeton* launched torpedoes against the dam and breached it.

Although the Royal Air Force played little part in the war, the Fleet Air Arm continued to provide a carrier presence and played a vital role in the United Nations strategy. The light carrier HMS *Theseus* as part of Task Force 77 was relieved by HMS *Glory* in April 1951 – this ship was in turn relieved by HMAS *Sydney*. These ships all carried Fairey Firefly and Hawker Sea Fury fighter-bombers. When HMS *Ocean* served in the theatre from May until October 1952, the ship launched 123 fighter-bomber sorties in a single day. It was a Sea Fury FB Mk 11 from *Ocean*, piloted by Lieutenant Peter Carmichael, that flew straight into the history books on August 9, 1952, when the aircraft destroyed a Communist MiG-15 in air-to-air combat. This was the first example of a jet being destroyed by a piston-engined fighter in air combat.

By the ceasefire of July 27, 1953, 12 different US carriers had served 27 tours in the Sea of Japan as part of the UN task force. During periods of intensive air action, up to four carriers were on station at the same time. A second carrier unit, Task Force 95, enforced a blockade in the Yellow Sea off the west coast of North Korea. Over 301,000 carrier strikes were flown during the Korean War: 255,545 by the aircraft of Task Force 77; 25,400 by the British and Commonwealth aircraft of Task Force 95; and 20,375 by the escort carriers of Task Force 95.

Carrier-based combat losses for the United States Navy and Marine Corps were 541 aircraft while Britain's Fleet Air Arm lost 86 aircraft in combat and the Australian Fleet Air Arm lost 15.

It was, however, the performance of the US Navy aircraft that proved so important in the history of naval air power. US Congress finally gave the US Navy funding for its 'supercarrier'.

ABOVE LEFT AND ABOVE: **Two views of Royal Navy carrier HMS *Ocean* with Fireflies and Sea Furies on the deck. *Ocean* was a Colossus-class light fleet carrier launched in July 1944, and on December 3, 1945, the ship became the first aircraft carrier to receive landings by a jet aircraft. The Royal Navy operated five carriers off Korea as part of the British and Commonwealth element of the United Nations forces and *Ocean* made two tours – May 5 to November 8, 1952, and the second from May 17, 1953, to the end of hostilities. It was during the first tour that Sea Fury pilot Lt Peter Carmichael from HMS *Ocean* achieved his historic victory over a MiG-15 jet** BELOW: **The Grumman F9F Panther was the US Navy's most widely used jet fighter in the conflict.** BOTTOM: **US Navy Corsairs on a snow-covered deck illustrate the challenging conditions in which deck crews and naval aviators have to operate.**

US Navy carriers and the Vietnam War

On August 2, 1964, the USS *Maddox*, a United States Navy destroyer carrying out electronic surveillance in the Tonkin Gulf, was attacked by North Vietnamese patrol boats. The US Navy presence was there in support of democratic South Vietnam, which Communist insurgents were entering from North Vietnam. The ultimate consequence of the attack was massive.

Five days later US Congress passed the Tonkin Gulf Resolution that authorized President Johnson to "take all necessary measures" to protect US interests. The carriers USS *Ticonderoga* and *Constellation* arrived in the area within days, and their jet aircraft launched bombing raids against North Vietnamese patrol boat bases and an oil storage depot.

Although the raids were judged to be a success, one aircraft was lost and its pilot, Lt Everett Alvarez Jr, became the first of around 600 downed US airmen who became prisoners of war. Alvarez was not released until the peace treaty was signed eight years later.

These raids, launched from US Navy aircraft carriers, were the first air missions of the Vietnam War. What followed until August 15, 1973, was the longest (nine years), most costly (in terms of aircraft and crews) and probably the most difficult war in naval aviation history.

During the war, US aircraft carriers were based in the South China Sea on 'Yankee Station' (off North Vietnam) and 'Dixie Station' (off South Vietnam) and provided air support for US forces fighting south of the Demilitarized Zone (DMZ) in the Republic of (South) Vietnam. The carriers also served as bases for USN aircraft operating on bombing missions over North Vietnam and Laos.

TOP: **Carrier-borne air power was fundamental to the US air war conducted over Vietnam. Without the carriers and the role the US Navy and Marine Corps played, the US effort would have been limited to missions conducted from land bases.**
ABOVE: **A US Navy F-4 Phantom II prepares to launch followed by a North American Vigilante. Both aircraft served in the conflict but the F-4 served with the US Air Force and US Marine Corps, as well as the US Navy in the war. The Phantom was used for fighter, bomber, reconnaissance and 'wild weasel' jamming missions.**

Aircraft crews were bound by political constraints and targets were chosen carefully to avoid any action that would provoke Chinese or Soviet intervention. Despite all the air warfare in the sky over Vietnam, only five US pilots (USAF and USN) achieved ace status. This was because North Vietnamese pilots were careful to avoid dogfighting. The rules of engagement also specified that US pilots had to have visual confirmation of any enemy aircraft before engaging. By this point it was too close for air-to-air missiles like Sidewinders to be effective and it was not until later in the war that fighters

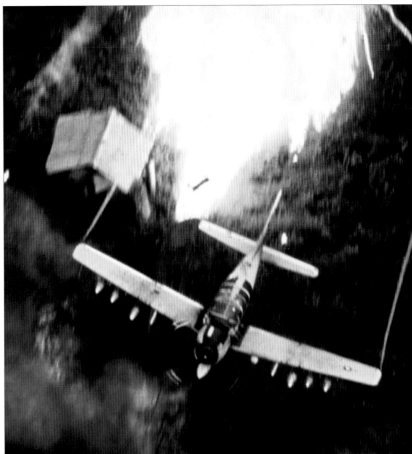

were armed with effective guns. American pilots were found overall to have lost the air-fighting skills that proved so vital in Korea and World War II. This led to the establishment of the Top Gun programme for US Navy pilots.

The US Navy crews were also operating against an enemy equipped with sophisticated Soviet anti-aircraft defences. In 1965, the North Vietnamese began building a massive Surface-to-Air Missile (SAM) arsenal. After US raids, these SAM sites were always the first to be rebuilt but the rules of engagement specified that US aircraft could only attack them if the sites were a minimum of 48km/30 miles from a city and had their radar turned on. The presence of the SAM sites led US pilots to fly low and fast below enemy radar with the result that some, flying the most advanced combat aircraft in the world, were brought down by small arms fire.

US Navy aircraft operating from carriers suffered heavy losses in the war. In 1968 alone, the USS *Oriskany* lost half of its air complement, 39 aircraft, in just 122 days, a staggering attrition rate. Carriers expected to lose on average 20 aircraft for each cruise in the theatre.

The number of carriers deployed varied during the conflict, but up to six operated at one time during Operation Linebacker. Twenty-one US aircraft carriers deployed under the US Seventh Fleet and conducted 86 war cruises for a total of 9,178 days on the line in the Gulf of Tonkin. A total of 530 aircraft were lost in combat, (most to surface-to-air missiles or anti-aircraft fire) and 329 more in operational accidents. In all, 377 US naval aviators lost their lives, 64 were reported missing and 179 were taken prisoners-of-war. A further 205 officers and men of the ships' crews of three carriers (*Forrestal*, *Enterprise*, and *Oriskany*) were killed in major shipboard fires caused by accidents, not enemy action, and many more were injured.

ABOVE LEFT: **The Douglas A-4 Skyhawk was a vital element in the US Navy's war. All carrier wings had Skyhawk squadrons and the A-4s performed many of the Navy's and Marine Corps' light air attack missions over the jungles and mountains of Vietnam. Production of this remarkable naval aircraft did not cease until 1979.** ABOVE: **Napalm was widely used in the Vietnam War, and in this photograph is dropped by a Douglas Skyraider. Essentially a sticky incendiary petrol jelly, the substance is formulated to burn at a specific rate and stick to whatever it hits. Napalm also rapidly deoxygenates available air and creates large amounts of carbon monoxide. Apart from its use against troops and buildings, Napalm bombs were also used in the Vietnam War to clear landing zones for helicopters.** BELOW: **The Douglas Skyraider, in this case the A-1H version, was widely used in Vietnam. The versatile aircraft bucked the trend of switching to jet aircraft and remained in front-line use long after its expected retirement date. US Navy Skyraiders were even credited with the destruction of two Soviet-built MiG-17 jet fighters during the war. The type flew on until November 1972 when it was replaced by the A-7 Corsair II.**

Naval aircraft armament since 1945

Even before World War II ended it was clear that the jet fighter aircraft that would develop would need more effective armament than the machine-guns then available, some of which were based on World War I designs. The closing speeds of two jet aircraft and the area over which a jet dogfight could take place meant that pilots might get one passing chance to down an enemy aircraft – guns had to pack real destructive power. At the end of World War II, German fighter armament development was considered the most advanced and some of their weapons were adopted and improved by the Allies after the war. The advanced Mauser MG-213 cannon, for example, was copied by Britain, Russia, the US, Switzerland and France among others, and equipped most of the world's air forces in the post-war period. The British version of the Mauser, the Aden, is still used today. Some aircraft, Dassault's Super Etendard and Rafale for example, are armed with even larger calibre guns like the 30mm GIAT/DEFA cannon, but even highly evolved cannon have their limitations and cannot be effective over great distances.

Aircraft-launched guided and unguided missiles were used in World War II but the single most important development in aircraft armament since the war has been the guided Air-to-Air Missile (AAM) with its high-explosive warhead. Unguided missiles, many of them of World War II vintage, continued to be used into the 1950s.

Guided AAMs are now used by fighters to attack enemy aircraft from a minimum of 1.6km/1 mile away and up to 160km/100 miles. AAMs were first used in anger in 1958 when Taiwanese F-86 Sabres clashed with MiG-15s of the People's Republic of China. Armed with early examples of the AIM-9 Sidewinder, the F-86s downed a number of Chinese MiGs with the new weapon.

TOP: **A Royal Navy Sea Harrier FA.2 armed with four AIM-120 AMRAAMs (Advanced Medium-Range Air-to-Air Missiles). Weighing 154kg/340lb, each missile uses an advanced solid-fuel rocket motor to reach a speed of Mach 4 and a range in excess of 48km/30 miles. The AIM-120 can counter the electronic jamming of an enemy and on intercept an active-radar proximity fuse detonates the 40lb high-explosive warhead to destroy the target.**
ABOVE: **The AGM-65 Maverick is an air-to-ground tactical missile used against armour, air defences, ships, vehicles and fuel storage facilities. Using infrared tracking, the missile has a range of 27km/17 miles and can carry a warhead of up to 135kg/300lb.**

Modern air-to-air missiles are usually Infra-Red (IR) guided (in which the missile sensors make it follow a high-temperature heat source such as an engine exhaust) or radar-guided (in which the missile homes in on a target illuminated by a radar from the aircraft, and then follows on its own radar). The latter type of missile normally uses a technique called semi-active radar homing, which allows the radar to operate in pulses, to

FAR LEFT: **Armed with six long-range Phoenix air-to-air missiles, the F-14 Tomcat was a formidable air combat adversary. The potent missiles weighing 447kg/ 985lb could streak towards targets at speeds in excess of Mach 5.**
LEFT: **Although modern combat aircraft like the F-18 Hornet/Super Hornet are still armed with guns, it is unlikely they would ever be used in a modern air-combat environment where missiles dominate.**

avoid making itself a target to radar-homing missiles. Some missiles use both the IR and radar guidance methods, being radar-guided to within a few miles' range, then IR-guided to terminate in destruction.

Whatever the guidance, the AAM must reach its target quickly as most only have enough fuel for a few minutes' run. In missiles with speeds of three or four times the speed of sound, the run can be counted in seconds.

AAMs are usually proximity armed, and having detected that they are within lethal range, explode without having to hit the target. This is to counter last-second evasive manoeuvres by the target aircraft and even if a missile just misses the target, the detonation will still cause substantial damage. Air-to-air missiles are categorized according to their range, into Short-Range Missiles (SRAAMs), Medium-Range Missiles (MRAAMs), and Long-Range Missiles (LRAAMs).

The SRAAM is designed for use in close air combat and distances up to 18km/11 miles, and a typical SRAAM would be the well-known and widely used American Sidewinder (AIM-9) series.

The MRAAM is mainly used to intercept targets beyond SRAAM range, and uses a radar homing system with a greater detection range and better all-weather properties than the infrared guidance system.

LRAAMs are truly remarkable weapons, and perhaps the most impressive of all was the Phoenix carried exclusively by the US Navy F-14 Tomcat. In its time the world's most sophisticated and expensive AAM, the Phoenix had a speed of five times the speed of sound, and could be launched from over 200km/124 miles distance from a target, before the F-14 had even appeared on an enemy aircraft radar screen.

With no real alternatives on the horizon, air-to-air missiles will remain the prime armament of naval and indeed land-based fighters for many years to come.

ABOVE: **A torpedo-armed Royal Navy Westland Wasp HAS.1, typifying the real destructive but versatile power that post-war helicopter development brought to naval military aviation. The light Wasp could carry two Mk 44 or 46 torpedoes or Mk 44 depth charges. Incredibly, it was also cleared to carry the WE177 272kg/600lb Nuclear Depth Bomb.** BELOW: **A Royal Navy Supermarine Scimitar could carry up to 96 unguided rockets. This large and heavy fighter could also carry four AGM-45 Bullpup air-to-ground missiles or four AIM-9 Sidewinder air-to-air missiles.**

Aircraft carriers of the Falklands War

When Argentine forces invaded the Falkland Islands in early April, 1982, Britain's Royal Navy had only two of its four aircraft carriers in service – HMS *Invincible* and HMS *Hermes*. It was, however, only due to these two carriers and the aircraft they carried, that Britain was able to win a conflict some 12,900km/8,000 miles away.

The 1960s and 70s had seen a gradual run down of Britain's carrier assets and, following a 1981 Defence Review, *Invincible* was to have been sold to Australia. *Hermes*, however, had undergone a £30 million refit and conversion to become a ski-ramp carrier capable of operating the new Sea Harrier fighters that were to prove so vital during the Falklands campaign. *Hermes*, the task force flagship, and *Invincible* both sailed from Portsmouth on April 5, 1982, after a rapid, remarkable and frantic period of preparation.

At this stage in the Cold War, *Invincible*'s air group typically consisted of nine Sea King HAS.5 Anti-Submarine Warfare (ASW) helicopters and perhaps just five Sea Harrier FRS.1 fighters. This was because the mission for which the ship had trained was that of anti-submarine warfare in the North Atlantic pitted against Soviet submarines. In this form of warfare, the ASW helicopters were the most important air assets while the Sea Harriers were there to deal with Soviet patrol aircraft that might have got too close to the carrier. The Falklands changed that and showed that even post-Imperial Britain still had to retain the capability to use carriers to project military power wherever needed around the world. After the Falklands, the typical Royal Navy carrier air group became three AEW Sea Kings, nine ASW Sea Kings and eight or nine Sea Harriers.

TOP: **The Royal Navy carriers HMS *Illustrious*, foreground, and HMS *Invincible* pictured in September 1982. *Invincible* and *Hermes* were the only British carriers available when the conflict developed.** ABOVE: **This picture of the hangar deck in a British carrier during the war epitomizes the versatility, organization and planning that is required to wage war from an aircraft carrier. Harriers, helicopters and troops all prepare for battle beneath the ship's armoured deck.**

Aircraft carriers were, however, not the only ships to carry aircraft during the Falklands war. The Ministry of Defence requisitioned many merchant navy ships to sail south to help retake the Falklands. Although some were converted for use as troop carriers or floating hospitals, several were also converted into basic aircraft carriers. The container ship SS *Atlantic Conveyer*, for example, had been laid up on the Mersey but was quickly taken to Devonport for conversion into a 'Harrier Carrier' and headed south. With containers stacked around the flight deck, the ship and others like it were able to operate the versatile V/STOL Sea Harrier. Unfortunately, on May 25, the *Atlantic Conveyer* was struck by an air-launched Exocet missile

FAR LEFT: **A Royal Navy Sea Harrier leaves the ski-ramp of HMS _Hermes_. Sea Harriers alone claimed 24 kills with no losses in air combat, although 2 were lost to ground fire and 4 in accidents. Fleet Air Arm unit 801 NAS achieved a sortie rate of 99 per cent for all missions tasked, fired 12 missiles, 3,000 rounds of 30mm cannon and dropped 56 bombs.** LEFT: **The biggest airborne threat to the British task force were the anti-shipping missiles carried by Argentine Super Etendards. The weapons proved deadly against a number of British ships.** BELOW: **Helicopters were a vital element of the British inventory and enabled troops and supplies to be moved ashore and around the Islands quickly. They were also used for covert operations and casualty evacuation as well as anti-submarine patrols.**

and was destroyed with the loss of twelve crew, three Chinook and six Wessex helicopters. During the conflict, Royal Navy helicopter support and assault ships had both also successfully landed Sea Harriers on their helicopter flight decks.

The Argentine Navy also had a carrier in operation during the Falklands war, the _Veinticinco De Mayo_. Formerly Royal Navy Light Fleet Carrier HMS _Venerable_, launched in December 1943, _Veinticinco De Mayo_ was acquired by Argentina in 1961. The deployment of four Royal Navy nuclear-powered 'hunter-killer' submarines and the subsequent sinking of the cruiser _General Belgrano_ kept most of the Argentine fleet including _Veinticinco De Mayo_ in Argentina's shallow coastal waters. Accordingly the carrier played little part in the conflict although some of her aircraft later flew raids while operating from mainland Argentina.

When the war was over, _Hermes_ sailed back to the UK on July 5 while _Invincible_ remained on station until July 29 when

she was relieved by her brand-new, hurriedly completed sister-ship _Illustrious_ on August 27, 1982. _Illustrious_ was in fact completed three months ahead of schedule and after the quickest of sea trials sailed south, commissioning on the way. _Hermes_ arrived back at Portsmouth on the July 21 while _Invincible_ got home on September 17, having spent 166 days at sea, at that point a record for continuous Royal Navy carrier operations.

The sale of _Invincible_ was then cancelled and the Australians were offered the older _Hermes_ instead. _Invincible_ went on to see operational duty again off the former Yugoslavia and later Iraq. _Hermes_ was decommissioned in 1984, laid up at Portsmouth until 1986 and was sold to the Indian Navy who commissioned the ship on May 12, 1987, having renamed her INS _Viraat_ (Giant). The _Viraat_ is the flagship of the Indian Navy. The _Veinticinco De Mayo_ was laid up in 1993 and was finally scrapped in India during 1999.

ABOVE: **The _Atlantic Conveyor_ 'Harrier Carrier' was a 15,000-ton Cunard roll-on roll-off container ship and is pictured here with Chinooks and a Sea Harrier landing on the deck. It was destroyed by an Exocet on May 25, 1982.**

ABOVE: **Britain fielded a mixed Harrier force during the Falklands War as seen in this carrier deck shot from the time. The Sea Harriers were tasked with air defence while the RAF Harriers were to specialize in ground attack.**

Naval aviation technology – 1945 to the present day

For most of the latter half of the 20th century, combat aircraft designers continued to do what their predecessors had done – improve performance through a better understanding of aerodynamics, more powerful engines and harnessing all available technology. Piston-engined fighters had virtually reached the end of their evolutionary line by 1945 although many remained in service for some years after the end of World War II. Jet-powered fighters began to make their mark towards the end of the war, and within a decade supersonic speeds were regularly achieved, albeit in dives. At the same time, the advent of nuclear weapons made the development of nuclear-capable carrier-borne jet aircraft a high carrier priority for land-based and carrier forces.

A greater understanding of 'area rule' – the design technique that produces a fuselage contour with the lowest possible transonic wave drag – came in the 1950s and helped aircraft designers break through the 'sound barrier' and produce aircraft capable of supersonic speeds in level flight.

Jet engine technology progressed rapidly in the 1950s resulting in engines like the Buccaneer's Rolls-Royce 5,035kg/11,100lb-thrust Spey. This engine generated more than twice the output of the Sea Hawk's 2,268kg/5,000lb Rolls-Royce Nene. Afterburner or reheat capability was developed in

TOP: **The development of the helicopter has given naval strategists much greater flexibility in the types of forces and responses they can create in times of tension. Here, Royal Navy Wessexes are seen landing on HMS *Bulwark* when it served as a commando carrier.**
ABOVE: **Space is always an issue on carriers, and among the features used to alleviate the problem is folding helicopter tails and rotor blades. The aircraft shown is a Sea King of the US Navy unit HS-5.**

the late 1940s to give fighters an emergency boost of energy if required. When a pilot engages afterburner, additional fuel is simply burned in the jetpipe to generate extra thrust. This does consume considerable amounts of fuel and is used sparingly.

At first, jet fighters continued to use the construction techniques and materials employed on piston-engined aircraft. With the dawn of high-speed flight and the extreme stresses places on an airframe, designers began to look beyond aluminium and magnesium alloys and used titanium alloys and specially developed steel. Carbon or graphite fibre composites are also now commonly used as they weigh half as much as aluminium alloys but have three times the strength. This major weight saving reduces the overall weight of combat aircraft and allows them to carry more fuel or weaponry.

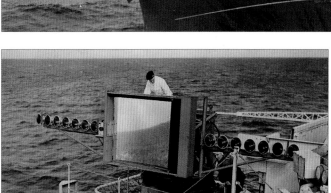

RIGHT: **Two aircraft designs, both capable of vertical take-off but very different – the Harrier family and the helicopter technically do not require conventional flight decks.** BELOW: **A Westland Wyvern pictured during tests of *Ark Royal*'s new steam catapult, which enabled heavier aircraft to operate from carriers.** BELOW RIGHT: **This system, the Mirror Landing Aid (MLA), replaced the earlier entirely human paddle-waving Deck Landing Officer system. Pilots of faster jets with a nose-up attitude struggled with the old system, so the British developed the MLA, which reflected the pilot's own landing lights back to him and, with mirrors and lenses, instructed him on his altitude and attitude.**

Jet-aircraft designers have always grappled with the problem of trying to reduce the take-off and landing runs of high-speed combat aircraft and never more so than on carrier operations. A truly innovative solution was the development of swing-wing, or variable geometry, in which the wings can move automatically from the swept to the spread position to maximize the aircraft's aerodynamic performance as required.

On take-off, the spread position generates more lift and gets the aircraft off the ground or carrier deck sooner. Once in the air, the wings can be swept back for high-speed performance. On approach to landing, the aircraft spreads its wings. As more lift is generated, the aircraft's speed slows, reducing the violence of the landing as the carrier aircraft's hook catches the wire. Only a handful of swing-wing combat aircraft have entered service and only one for carrier operations – the F-14 Tomcat.

The ultimate solution to the short take-off requirement is the Harrier – the only single-engined Vertical or Short Take-Off and Landing (V/STOL) in service. The key to the Harrier's truly remarkable vertical take-off capability lies with the vectored thrust from the Harrier's Rolls-Royce Pegasus engine, directed by four jet nozzles. The nozzles swivel as one, directing thrust from directly to the rear to just forward of vertical. In air combat the nozzles can be used to rapidly decelerate the aircraft so that an enemy aircraft, previously on the Harrier's tail, shoots by, unable to stop thus becoming the Harrier's prey instead. The Soviet Union developed the Harrier-inspired Yak-38 which became the first Soviet combat aircraft designed purely for carrier operation to enter series production and also the first production

ABOVE: **During 1985 the first outline design for a navalized version of the Su-27 fighter was developed from a design first approved in 1985. The Su-27K (K for *korabelny* or shipborne) but later designated the Su-33, was conceived to provide the Soviet Navy's new carriers with a fighter for self-defence. The aircraft is a late example of a landplane design being modified for carrier use.**

vertical take-off/landing aircraft built by the Soviet Union. While the Harrier had one versatile engine, the Yak-38 had an engine in the rear used for forward flight while two other smaller, less powerful engines were housed to the rear of the cockpit.

Where fighters once had mechanical linkages from control columns to control surfaces, modern fighters have Fly-By-Wire (FBW). This form of electronic signalling eliminates the need for mechanical linkages and a control column. Computers are now as fundamental to naval and land-based combat aircraft as engines and weapons.

Target – Libya

In 1986, following a number of terrorist attacks on US citizens and interests, US intelligence cited "incontrovertible" evidence that the incidents were sponsored by Libya. Meanwhile, the US Sixth Fleet based in the Mediterranean, began a series of manoeuvres designed to keep the pressure on Libya. Two, sometimes three, aircraft carriers (the *Saratoga, America* and *Coral Sea*) conducted 'freedom of navigation' operations that would take the US warships up to and then southward through a line across the sea that Libya's leader Colonel Gaddafi had proclaimed to be the "line of death".

ABOVE: **The USS *Saratoga* was one of the US Navy carriers on station in the region at the time of the tension with Libya. During the exchanges the ship launched A-7s armed with AGM-88 missiles, A-6s armed with AGM-84 missiles and Mk 20 Rockeye II cluster bombs, and EA-6Bs from VAQ-132.**
BELOW LEFT: **The picture shows an aircrew pre-flight briefing taking place onboard the *Saratoga* on March 22, 1986.**

The line marked the northernmost edge of the Gulf of Sidra and the Libyan leader had warned foreign vessels that the Gulf belonged to Libya and was not international waters – they entered at their own risk and were open to attack by Libyan forces. On March 24, 1986, Libyan air defence SAM missiles were launched against two US Navy F-14s intercepting an intruding Libyan MiG-25 that was too close to the US battle group. Next day, a Navy A-7E aircraft struck the SAM site with AGM-88A HARM missiles. At least two of five threatening Libyan naval attack vessels were also sunk.

US President Ronald Reagan wanted to mount a strike against the Libyan leader's regime but sought cooperation from Western allies. The USAF's plans assumed that UK-based F-111s could fly through French airspace to strike at Libya. Speculation about the strike in the Western media alerted the Libyans and caused the plan to be changed to include support aircraft (EF-111 and US Navy A-7 and EA-6B) to carry out suppression of enemy defences. The US Navy role in the operation grew as the raid had to hit Gaddafi hard.

ABOVE: **A US Navy pilot pictured with his A-7 Corsair II.** RIGHT: **A US Air Force F-111 takes off from RAF Lakenheath in Suffolk, England, heading for the attack on Libya after a 7-hour flight and a number of refuellings. Co-ordination was crucial for the attack involving US Navy, US Marine Corps and USAF aircraft.**

Plans were further complicated when France, Germany, Italy and Spain all refused to cooperate in a strike. The F-111s now had to navigate over the ocean around France and Spain, pass east over the Straits of Gibraltar, and then over the Mediterranean to line up for their bombing run on Libya. It would be a gruelling round-trip of 10,300km/6,400 miles taking 13 hours. On April 14, 1986, the United States launched Operation 'El Dorado Canyon' against Libya.

US planners tabled a joint USAF/USN operation against five major Libyan targets. Two were in Benghazi: a terrorist training camp and a military airfield. The other three targets were in Tripoli: a terrorist naval training base; the former Wheelus AFB; and the Azziziyah Barracks compound, which housed the HQ of Libyan intelligence and also contained one of five residences that Gaddafi was known to have used. Eighteen F-111s were to strike the Tripoli targets, while US Navy aircraft were to hit the two Benghazi sites.

At 17:36 GMT on April 14, 24 F-111s left the UK, six of them spare aircraft set to return after the first refuelling. The US Navy attack aircraft came from carriers of the US Sixth Fleet operating in the Mediterranean. *Coral Sea* provided eight A-6E medium bombers and six F/A-18C Hornets for strike support. USS *America* launched six A-6Es plus six A-7Es and an EA-6B for strike support. They faced a hazardous flight as Libya's air defence system was very sophisticated and virtually on a par with that of the Soviet Union. Timing was critical, and the USAF and USN attacks had to be simultaneous to maximize the element of surprise so that the strike aircraft could get in and out as quickly as possible. Of the eighteen F-111s that headed for Libya, five had aborted en route so at around midnight GMT, thirteen F-111s reached Tripoli and carried out their attack at speeds around 740kph/460mph and heights of 61m/200ft.

EF-111As and US Navy A-7s, A-6Es, and an EA-6B armed with HARM and Shrike anti-radar missiles flew in defence-suppression roles for the F-111s. Across the Gulf of Sidra, Navy A-6E aircraft attacked the Al Jumahiriya Barracks at Benghazi, and to the east, the Benina airfield. News of the attack was being broadcast in the US while it was underway. The Navy's Intruders destroyed four MiG-23s, two Fokker F-27s, and two Mil Mi-8 helicopters.

The operation was never intended to topple Gaddafi, but he was known to have been very shaken when bombs exploded near him. When he next appeared on state television he was certainly subdued. Most importantly, the raids demonstrated that even in those pre-stealth days and thanks to the support of aircraft carrier assets, the US had the capability to send its high-speed bombers over great distances to carry out precision attacks. The raid was considered a success, but the situation between the US and Gaddafi remained unresolved for another 17 years before an uneasy peace was agreed.

ABOVE: **Although the Libyan Air Force had the high-performance MiG-25 fighter, as pictured, no fighter opposition was encountered during the US attacks. Anti-aircraft defences were, however, extensive and resulted in the loss of one USAF F-111 shot down over the Gulf of Sidra.**

ABOVE: **A Libyan Air Force Sukhoi Su-22 of the kind Libya operated at the time. The defences the attacking US aircraft did encounter were sophisticated long-range anti-aircraft missiles. Tripoli alone was protected by an estimated 214 anti-aircraft missiles at the time.**

A 21st-century carrier at war

A recent deployment of the United States Navy carrier USS *Enterprise* – 'the Big E' – is a good illustration of the nature, scale and capability of current US naval air power. On November 18, 2006, more than 5,400 sailors assigned to USS *Enterprise* (CVN-65) returned to Naval Station Norfolk, Virginia, following a six-month deployment in support of the ongoing rotation of forward-deployed forces conducting "operations in support of the global war on terrorism".

Nuclear-powered aircraft carrier USS *Enterprise* was deployed on May 2, 2006, as the flagship of *Enterprise* Carrier Strike Group (ENT CSG) comprised of Carrier Air Wing One (CVW-1), Destroyer Squadron Two (DESRON-2), USS *Enterprise* (CVN 65), guided-missile cruiser USS *Leyte Gulf* (CG 55), guided-missile destroyer USS *McFaul* (DDG 74), guided-missile frigate USS *Nicholas* (FFG 47), and fast combat support ship USS *Supply* (T-AOE 6). On its cruise, the carrier supported operations in the US 5th, 6th and 7th Fleet areas of responsibility.

Carrier Air Wing (CVW) 1, embarked on the *Enterprise* included the 'Sidewinders' of Strike Fighter Squadron (VFA) 86, the 'Checkmates' of VFA-211, the 'Knighthawks' of VFA-136, the 'Thunderbolts' of Marine Strike Fighter Squadron (VMFA) 251, the 'Screwtops' of Airborne Early Warning Squadron (VAW) 123, the 'Rooks' of Tactical Electronic Warfare Squadron (VAQ) 137, the 'Maulers' of Sea Control Squadron (VS) 32, the 'Rawhides' of Carrier Logistics Support (VRC) 40, and the 'Dragonslayers' of Helicopter Anti-Submarine Squadron (HS) 11.

During the cruise, the squadrons of CVW-1 flew nearly 23,000 hours, including nearly 12,000 hours of combat

TOP: **The nuclear-powered aircraft carrier USS *Enterprise* (CVN 65) pulls into its homeport of Naval Station Norfolk, after a six-month deployment. The *Enterprise* was commissioned in November 1961 and is 342m/1,123ft long. It was built to accommodate 99 aircraft and its nuclear power provides steam for the operation of four catapults. It was completed with an all-missile armament.**
ABOVE: **An F/A-18C Hornet, attached to the 'Checkmates' of Strike Fighter Squadron Two One One, prepares to 'shoot' off the flight deck of the *Enterprise*.**

missions in Operations 'Iraqi Freedom' and 'Enduring Freedom'. During its deployment, the *Enterprise* steamed nearly 100,000km/60,000 miles, dropped 137 precision weapons over nearly 8,500 sorties flown, and spent nearly $10 million alone on feeding the crew. Around 15.6 million emails were sent and received aboard the *Enterprise*.

"Carrier Air Wing 1 and the entire *Enterprise* Strike Group team were prepared to flexibly and effectively support a variety of missions," said Captain Mark Wralstad, Commander, CVW-1. "Whether we operated carrier-based aircraft from

ABOVE LEFT: **An F/A-18C Hornet clears the** *Enterprise* **deck. Armed with a 20mm cannon and up to 7,000kg/15,500lb of weapons including air-to-air missiles, other guided weapons and rockets and tactical nuclear weapons, the Hornet is one of the world's most capable combat aircraft.** ABOVE: **The** *Enterprise* **displaces 89,600 tons and at the commissioning was the world's first nuclear-powered aircraft carrier and simply the mightiest warship to ever sail the seas.** *Enterprise* **is the tallest (76m/250ft) carrier in the US Navy and the fastest. The picture shows personnel gathering on the bow for a vital FOD (Foreign Object Damage) walk on the flight deck as the ship passes through the Suez Canal.** LEFT: **Sailors aboard the** *Enterprise* **direct an HH-60H Seahawk helicopter, attached to the 'Dragonslayers' of Helicopter Anti-submarine Squadron (HS) 11, on the flight deck during a vertical replenishment (VERTREP) with the Military Sealift Command (MSC) fleet replenishment oiler USNS** *Laramie.*

land, engaged our nation's enemies from the sea, or engaged our friends and allies from the flight deck of *Enterprise*, the entire strike group helped to set the conditions for security and stability throughout the world."

During June and July 2006, *Enterprise* aircraft launched 781 aircraft sorties in direct support of troops participating in Operation 'Iraqi Freedom' and 237 aircraft sorties in support of Operation 'Enduring Freedom'.

On one day alone, September 20, 2006, aircraft assigned to CVW-1 stationed aboard USS *Enterprise* flew 14 missions in the skies over Afghanistan and provided their heaviest day of close air support to International Security Assistance Force (ISAF) troops and other coalition forces on the ground as part of Operation 'Enduring Freedom'.

F/A-18F Super Hornets from the 'Checkmates' of Strike Fighter Squadron (VFA) 211, supported both ISAF and other coalition ground forces in multiple locations north of Kandahar in Afghanistan. The Navy's latest generation of fighter/attack aircraft completed multiple strafing runs against the Taliban using the aircraft's M61A1 20mm Gatling gun and ended the engagement by dropping Guided Bomb Unit (GBU)-12 weapons – general-purpose, laser-guided 226kg/500lb bombs.

Later that day, the *Enterprise*-based 'Checkmates' attacked a compound north of Kandahar believed to be a Taliban haven.

The compound was destroyed with GBU-12 weapons. After refuelling, 'Checkmates' aircraft flew multiple show-of-force missions north of Kandahar against the Taliban who were attacking coalition ground forces with small arms fire.

F/A-18C Hornets from the 'Sidewinders' of VFA-86 performed multiple strafing runs against Taliban positions near Kandahar. The *Enterprise*-based aircraft expended GBU-12 weapons against the extremists, ending the engagement.

The 'Sidewinders' continued their missions later that day as they provided support for ISAF ground convoys and coalition troops. When ground controllers notified the *Enterprise*-based aircraft of a Taliban compound used for offensive action against ISAF and coalition ground forces identified north of Kandahar, 'Sidewinders' Hornet aircraft expended multiple GBU-12 weapons against the fortification, destroying the target.

Speaking at the time, Rear Admiral Raymond Spicer, commander of the *Enterprise* Carrier Strike Group, said, "Whether *Enterprise* strike group is protecting coalition troops on the ground, conducting planned strikes on known terrorist sites, or providing airborne command and control for our coalition partners, we have demonstrated our ability to operate as a combat-ready naval force capable of sustained combat operations, deterring aggression, preserving freedom of the seas, and promoting peace and security."

Current and future carriers

Today, aircraft carriers remain the largest military ships operated by modern navies. By way of example, a US Navy Nimitz-class carrier, powered by a combination of two nuclear reactors and four steam turbines, is 333m/1,092ft long and costs about US$4.5 billion. The United States Navy is the world's largest carrier operator with eleven in service, one under construction, and one on order. It is these warships that are the cornerstone of the United States' ability to 'project power' around the world. During the 2003 invasion of Iraq, US aircraft carriers served as the primary base of US air power. As a result, and even without the ability to place significant numbers of aircraft on land bases, the United States was capable of carrying out significant air attacks from carrier-based squadrons. Although nations including Britain and France are looking to increase their carrier capability, the US will remain the dominant carrier operator.

At the time of writing, ten countries maintain a total of 20 aircraft carriers in active service. As well as the USA, Britain, France, Russia, Italy, India, Spain, Brazil, Thailand and China all have carriers that operate or are capable of operations. In addition, South Korea, Britain, Canada, China, India, Japan, Australia, Chile, Singapore and France also operate naval

TOP: **A BAE SYSTEMS proposed early design for the next generation of Royal Navy aircraft carriers, the CVF. Large new carriers require massive investment to bring into service and take so long to develop that the threat they are developed to counter can change in the meantime.**
ABOVE: **The USS *Abraham Lincoln* (CVN-72) boasts all the amenities found in any American city with a comparable population. These include a post office (with its own post or 'zip' code), TV and radio stations, newspaper, fire department, library, hospital, general store, barber shops, and more.**

vessels capable of carrying and operating significant numbers of military helicopters.

Using techniques developed during World War II, aircraft carriers never cruise alone and are generally accompanied by a variety of other warships that provide protection for the carrier, which would be a prime target for any potential enemy. The collection of ships, with the carrier at its heart, is known as a battle group, carrier group or carrier battle group.

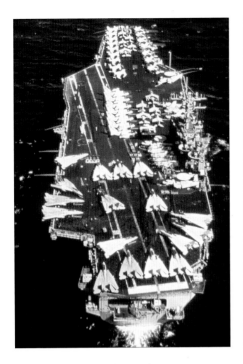

The Royal Navy plans to replace its current carrier fleet of three Invincible-class carriers operating Harriers and helicopters with two new larger STOVL 'CVF' aircraft carriers. HMS *Queen Elizabeth* and HMS *Prince of Wales* are scheduled to enter service in 2014 and 2016 respectively. Each ship will be a similar size and weight as the ocean liner the QE2. A CVF would weigh 65,000 tons (around 32,500 average family cars) at full displacement and measure 284m/931ft in length with a flight-deck width of 73m/239ft. With nine decks, the flight-deck could handle a maximum of 40 aircraft (36 Joint Strike Fighters and 4 AEW aircraft) and would be compatible with the aircraft of friendly nations. Each of the two huge lifts that move aircraft from hangar to flight deck can carry two aircraft apiece and are so big just one of them could carry the weight of the entire ship's crew.

A CVF will carry over 8,600 tons of fuel to support the ship and its aircraft, which would be enough for the average family car to travel to the moon and back 12 times. Crew numbers will be just 40 per cent larger than those of the current Royal Navy carriers although the new ships will be three times larger. The two ships will be the largest warships ever built for the Royal Navy.

Despite all the shipbuilding advances, improvements in the technology and capabilities of anti-ship missiles mean that the vulnerability of carriers will always be a concern for naval strategists. Though the carrier and the carrier group can defend itself against multiple threats, in time, the prime ships of navies may well become submarines. Already capable of unleashing formidable nuclear and conventional firepower, submarines remain difficult to attack when operating deep in the ocean. Although these submarines could launch and retrieve unmanned reconnaissance aircraft (drones), there would be no place for manned aircraft and naval aviation as we know it could become a matter for history books and aviation museums.

ABOVE LEFT: **The Nimitz-class supercarriers are a class of five nuclear-powered aircraft carriers in service with the US Navy and are the largest capital ships in the world. The ships are numbered with consecutive hull numbers starting with CVN-68. The letters CVN denote the type of ship – CV is the hull classification for aircraft carriers, while N indicates nuclear propulsion. The number after the CVN means that this is the 68th aircraft carrier.**
ABOVE: **USS *Enterprise* (CVAN-65) is manoeuvred by tugs in shallow water.**
BELOW: ***Charles de Gaulle* (R91) is France's only serving aircraft carrier and is the flagship of the French Navy. It is the first French nuclear-powered surface vessel, and the first nuclear-powered carrier built for an operator other than the United States Navy.** BOTTOM: ***Admiral Kuznetsov* was launched in 1985 and was commissioned into the Soviet Navy but is now the flagship of the Russian Navy. The carrier has no catapult so cannot launch aircraft with heavy offensive loads but has got a ski-ramp.**

Top Gun

Immortalized by the 1986 Hollywood blockbuster of the same name, Top Gun, or more properly the United States Navy Fighter Weapons School (NFWS) was established in 1969. Although no longer based at Miramar in California or flying F-14s, the current incarnation of Top Gun remains a vital means of keeping the US Navy at the forefront of air fighting doctrine.

In the early years of the Vietnam war, the United States was not achieving the same level of air-to-air combat superiority that it had enjoyed in Korea. By 1968, concerns about the comparatively low kill ratio in South-east Asia prompted the formation of a US Navy air combat 'masters' course teaching Air Combat Manoeuvring (ACM) and weapons systems use. The first course commenced on March 3, 1969, and Top Gun was formally commissioned as a separate command at NAS Miramar on July 7, 1972. From then on, NFWS became the hub for Navy and Marine Corps tactics development and training. The school focused on teaching the art of Dissimilar Air Combat Manoeuvring using 'friendly' aircraft to replicate the handling and capabilities of enemy aircraft such as the MiG-17 and MiG-21.

Top Gun instructors initially operated the A-4 Skyhawk to replicate the MiG-17 and borrowed USAF T-38 Talons to 'be' the MiG-21 to instruct F-4 Phantom aircrews in dissimilar training. Top Gun swiftly established itself as a centre of excellence in fighter doctrine, tactics and training and soon every US Navy fighter squadron had its share of Top Gun graduates who served as Subject Matter Experts (SMEs) in their units passing on their expertise. US Navy win-to-loss ratios in South-east Asia climbed to 20:1 before standardizing at the target level of 12.5:1. The USAF, without a Top Gun

LEFT: **The expression 'Top Gun' is now used around the world in military aviation, and has come to epitomize, as the Hollywood blockbuster film starring Tom Cruise stated, the best of the best. The Top Gun programme keeps the US Navy's pilots among the best fighting aviators in the world.**

programme of its own, maintained its poor kill-to-loss ratio until it too set up a dissimilar air combat training programme of their own. Successful Top Gun graduates who achieved air combat victories over North Vietnam and returned to Top Gun as instructors included 'Mugs' McKeown, Jack Ensch and the first US 'aces' of the Vietnam War, Randy 'Duke' Cunningham and Willie Driscoll.

With the 1970s and 1980s came the introduction of the Grumman F-14 and the Northrop F/A-18 Hornet as the US Navy's primary fleet fighter aircraft flown by Top Gun students. Meanwhile, Top Gun instructors retained their A-4s and F-5s, but also added the General Dynamics F-16 to more accurately simulate the threat posed by the Soviet Union's latest MiG-29 and Sukhoi Su-27 fighters. During the 1990s, the students' syllabus was developed with greater emphasis on the air-to-ground strike mission to reflect the real missions flown by multi-role aircraft like the F-14 and F/A-18. Eventually the

ABOVE: **Twenty-five modified Israeli Kfir-C1s were leased to the US Navy and the US Marine Corps from 1985 to 1989 to act as adversary aircraft in dissimilar air combat training. Of these aircraft, which were designated F-21A Lion, the 12 F-21 aircraft leased to the US Navy were painted in a three-tone blue-gray 'ghost' scheme and were operated by VF-43, based at NAS Oceana. In 1988 they were returned and replaced by the F-16N.**

BELOW: **The now retired F-14 Tomcat, here shown with wings sweeping back, was one of the world's greatest combat aircraft. Top Gun made very good pilots even better.**
RIGHT: **A Tomcat with its wings spread and 'fires burning' just after take-off. The final Tomcat Top Gun class graduated in early October 2003 and the type was retired from US Navy service in 2006.**

instructors retired their A-4s and F-5s, which were replaced by F-14s and F/A-18s.

1996 saw the end of an era when Top Gun left its California base and was absorbed into the Naval Strike and Air Warfare Center (NSAWC) at NAS Fallon, Nevada. Today's Top Gun instructors fly the F/A-18A/B/C Hornet and the F-16A/B Falcon (aircraft destined for Pakistan but never delivered due to embargoes) that are assigned to NSAWC. Top Gun continues to refine fighter tactics in its Power Projection and Maritime Air Superiority modules to keep the Fleet aware of and trained in current tactical developments.

There are five courses each year, each 6 weeks in duration for 12 US Fleet fighter and strike fighter aircrews. This course is designed to train experienced US Navy and Marine Corps fighter aircrews at an advanced level in all aspects of fighter aircraft use including tactics, hardware, techniques, and the 'current world threat'. The course includes around 80 hours of lectures and a rigorous flight syllabus that sets student aircrews against adversary aircraft flown by Top Gun instructors. Just as Top Gun was originally conceived, each new graduate of the Navy Fighter Weapons School returns to their operational squadron as a training officer fully trained in the latest tactical doctrine.

Top Gun also runs an Adversary Training Course, flying with adversary aircrew from each Navy and Marine Corps adversary squadron. These pilots receive individual instruction in threat simulation, effective threat presentation, and adversary tactics.

Tactics being developed today at the US Navy Fighter Weapons School will enable US Navy aircrews to carry an aggressive and successful fight to the enemy and ensure that they remain Top Guns.

ABOVE: **Feeling the need for speed, an F-14 flies in formation with an A-4 Skyhawk, the latter being the favoured mount of Top Gun instructors for a number of years.** BELOW: **The A-4 had comparable handling to the MiG-17 and was a vital teaching aid used for tutoring the pilots who could have faced the best aviators the Warsaw Pact and other potential enemies could muster.**

An A–Z of Modern Naval Aircraft

Since the end of World War II, naval aviation development has been dominated by high-performance jet-powered carrier-borne aircraft. Jets soon replaced the piston-powered fighters in the post-war front line. The wartime realization that the best naval aircraft were those developed specifically for carrier operations was embraced by aircraft designers.

The fast 'Top Gun' jet-engined types are not, however, the only naval aircraft. Carrier-borne AEW aircraft like the Gannet and Tracker were developed as were incredibly important aircraft such as the Grumman Intruder. Technological developments have seen the introduction, albeit limited, of Vertical/Short Take-Off and Landing (V/STOL) aircraft, namely the Harrier family and the Yak-38. Helicopters have grown in their importance in the period while the large flying boat has all but died out with a few notable exceptions, including the ShinMaywa SS-2.

The next generation of true carrier aircraft will be entering large-scale service soon and they will replace the aircraft developed to fight in the Cold War. The very different world stage demands a different response from the world's naval air arms and the new crop of aircraft like the Lockheed Martin Lightning II will put even venerable types like the F-14 Tomcat in the shade with their integrated applications of the latest technologies.

LEFT: **For many, the definitive modern naval aircraft was the Grumman F-14 Tomcat. Now retired, this high-performance aircraft was just one of many and varied types – both fixed and rotary wing – that comprised late 20th-century naval air power.**

Agusta Westland EH 101 Merlin

The Merlin, one of the world's most capable medium-sized helicopters, resulted from a 1977 Naval Staff requirement describing a new ASW helicopter needed to replace the Westland Sea King in service with the Royal Navy. By late 1977 Westland started work on design studies to meet this requirement. At the same time in Italy, the Italian Navy and Italian helicopter company Agusta were considering the replacement of the Agusta-built Sea Kings then in service. Inter-company discussions led to a joint venture agreement between the companies and the countries. In June 1980 a joint company, European Helicopter Industries (EHI), was set up to manage the project, by then designated the EH 101.

Manufacture of the first parts began in March 1985 at Yeovil and at Cascina Costa near Milan. The first prototype, PP1 (British military serial ZF641), was rolled out at Yeovil on April 7, 1987, and after exhaustive ground testing, first flew on October 9, 1987. The second pre-production example, PP2, flew soon after in Italy on November 26, 1987. Assembly of the Merlin began in early 1995, and the first production example flew on December 6, 1995. The Royal Navy received its first fully operational Merlin HM.1 on May 27, 1997, for trials.

The first of 22 examples for the RAF left the factory in November 1999. Designated Merlin HC.3 and sharing the same RTM.322 engines as the Royal Navy examples, the RAF Merlin is a utility version. The Italian Navy received its first production EH 101 in January 2001.

The Merlin HM Mk 1 has been in service with the Royal Navy, its main operator, since 1998 and although primarily employed as an anti-submarine helicopter, the Merlin can also participate in anti-surface warfare. The Merlin is designed to operate from both large and small ship flight decks, in severe weather and high sea states, by day or night. Overall

ABOVE: **A Royal Navy Merlin in flight. Despite a protracted development programme, the EH 101 is now considered to be one of the world's most capable medium-sized helicopters, and export orders are increasing.**
LEFT: **Perhaps the greatest export achievement was the adoption of a US-built version, the VH-71, as the 'Marine One' Presidential Helicopter Replacement programme aircraft.**

dimensions are less than those of a Sea King, and when embarked at sea, British examples can operate primarily from any ship with a capable flight deck.

Powered by three Rolls-Royce/Turbomeca gas turbines, the rugged, crashworthy airframe is of modular construction and is composed mainly of conventional aluminium-alloy construction with some composite materials in the rear fuselage and tail section. The naval version has powered main rotor blade folding and tail rotor pylon folding. All versions can fly in severe icing and incorporate triple hydraulic systems, three independent alternators and a gas turbine auxiliary power unit.

The aircraft and its mission system are managed by two computers, linked by dual data buses. All crew stations can access the management computers and can operate the tactical displays, fed by the Blue Kestrel radar. Navigation is state of the art with ring laser gyros, inertial reference systems GPS, Doppler and radar altimeters. The avionics include a digital flight control system, a glass cockpit with colour Multi-Function Displays and a comprehensive navigation suite for

RIGHT: **The Merlin HM Mk 1 has been in service with the Royal Navy since 1998. There are five Squadrons, 814 820, 829, 824 and 700, and all are based at the Royal Naval Air Station Culdrose in Cornwall when disembarked.**
FAR RIGHT: **The Canadian Air Force's only dedicated search-and-rescue (SAR) helicopter is the CH-149 Cormorant variant of the Merlin.**

all-weather navigation and automatic flight. Royal Navy Merlins have the Ferranti/Thomson-CSF dipping sonar.

The Merlin's operational debut came in early 2003 when four aircraft from 814 NAS embarked aboard RFA *Fort Victoria* were deployed into the northern Gulf as part of the UK Amphibious Task Group for Operation 'Iraqi Freedom'. With no submarine threat, the helicopters were used in an anti-surface warfare role protecting against swarm attacks by small, fast inshore attack craft. With no ASW requirement, the aircraft's Active Dipping Sonar (ADS) was removed to free up space in the cabin for an extra eight seats to be fitted plus racks for four stretchers. A 7.62mm general-purpose machine-gun was also fitted in the forward starboard window, and a semi-automatic cargo release unit for loading and vertical replenishment or air drops.

As well as Britain and Italy, naval Merlins are also operated by Japan, Portugal and Canada.

ABOVE: **The EH 101 is equipped with chaff and flare dispensers, directed infrared countermeasures infrared jammers, missile approach warners, and a laser detection and warning system.** BELOW LEFT: **It is rumoured that the EH 101 designation was a typing error that stuck as the aircraft was to be called EHI-01.**

Agusta Westland Merlin HM.1

First flight: October 9, 1987 (prototype)
Power: Three Rolls-Royce/Turbomeca 2,312shp RTM.322-01 turboshafts
Armament: Two hard points, one on each side of the fuselage, can carry up to 960kg/2,116lb of homing torpedoes, sonobuoy dispensers or anti-ship missiles
Size: Rotor diameter – 18.59m/61ft
Length – 22.81m/74ft 10in
Height – 6.65m/21ft 10in
Weights: Empty – 10,500kg/23,149lb
Maximum take-off –14,600kg/32,188lb
Performance: Maximum speed – 309kph/192mph
Service ceiling – 4,575m/15,000ft
Range – 925km/574 miles
Climb – 612m/2,008ft per minute

Armstrong Whitworth (Hawker) Sea Hawk

The graceful Sea Hawk is remarkable for three reasons – it was Hawker's first jet fighter, the first standard jet fighter of Britain's Fleet Air Arm and it remained in front-line service long after swept-wing fighters equipped navies elsewhere. Its layout was also unusual in that the seemingly twin-engined type in fact had a single jet pipe bifurcated (split) to feed two exhaust ducts, one at each trailing edge wing root. The leading edge wing roots included the two corresponding air intakes.

The Sea Hawk was derived from the Hawker P.1040, an aircraft built speculatively by the company, which flew in September 1947 and was proposed as a new fighter for both the Royal Navy and the Royal Air Force. Only the Navy placed orders for the Sea Hawk and after only building 35 production Sea Hawk fighters, Hawker transferred production to Armstrong Whitworth, hence the occasional confusion over the Sea Hawk manufacturer's identity. As a design the Sea Hawk certainly looked right, coming from the same team that designed the Hurricane and, later, the Hunter.

The first Royal Navy Sea Hawk squadron, No.806, formed in March 1953 carrying its distinctive ace of diamonds logo on its Sea Hawk Mk 1s. Later that year, one of the squadron's Sea

ABOVE: **The Royal Navy Historic Flight's Sea Hawk WV908 was built in late 1954 as an FGA.4 variant and 'joined' the Royal Navy in February 1955. After service with 807 Squadron and then 898 Squadron it embarked on HMS *Ark Royal* and HMS *Bulwark*.** BELOW LEFT: **Sea Hawks of No.806 NAS.**

Hawks, flown by Lieutenant Commander Chilton on to USS *Antietam,* became the first British aircraft to land on a fully angled carrier deck. In February the following year, 806 embarked on HMS *Eagle.* The Mk 2, of which 40 examples were built, had fully powered aileron controls but shared the same Rolls-Royce Nene 101 engine as the Mk 1.

The most widely used Sea Hawk version was the Mk 3 fighter bomber, capable of carrying considerable amounts of ordnance (two 227kg/500lb bombs or mines) under its strengthened wings. The 97 FGA Mk 4 versions built were optimized for the close air support role and could carry four 227kg/500lb bombs or up to sixteen 3in/76mm rocket projectiles with 27kg/60lb warheads. This change in usage was due to the realization that the Sea Hawk's performance could not match that of potential enemies in air-to-air combat. Re-engined (with the 5,200lb thrust Nene 103), Mks 3 and 4 became Mks 5 and 6 respectively. A further 86 Mk 6s were newly produced from the factory.

That said, the Fleet Air Arm's Sea Hawks did see action in the ground-attack role during the 1956 Suez Crisis. On the morning of November 1, 1956, the first Anglo-French carrier-launched attacks against Egyptian airfields began with 40 Royal Navy Sea Hawks and Sea Venoms launched from British carriers. Sea Hawks from HMS *Eagle*, *Albion* and *Bulwark* all saw action during the politically disastrous 'crisis' during which two were shot down, but the type was proven as a combat-capable ground-attack aircraft.

LEFT: **The straight-winged Sea Hawk flew on in front-line service after being 'reinvented' as a fighter-bomber.** ABOVE: **This Sea Hawk was built as an F.1 by Hawker. Note the folded wings and the auxiliary fuel tanks.**

The type continued in front-line FAA service until 1960, but some continued in second-line roles until 1969. Some ex-Royal Navy aircraft were supplied to the Royal Australian and Canadian navies, but the biggest export customers were the German naval air arm, the Netherlands and the Indian Navy. Dutch aircraft were equipped to carry an early version of the Sidewinder air-to-air missile until their phasing-out in 1964. German Sea Hawks operated exclusively from land bases in the air defence role until the mid-1960s. The Indian Navy's Sea Hawks saw action in the war with Pakistan in 1971 and soldiered on, remarkably, into the mid-1980s when they were replaced by Sea Harriers. The Royal Navy's Historic Flight maintains a lone Sea Hawk FGA Mk 4 in airworthy condition that is much in demand at UK air shows.

ABOVE RIGHT: **VP413 was one of three Hawker P.1040 Sea Hawk prototypes used to test the design and its military potential.** ABOVE: **The sole flying Sea Hawk shows the type's clean lines. Note the arrester hook and the excellent view from the cockpit, essential for deck landings.**

Armstrong Whitworth (Hawker) Sea Hawk F. Mk 1

First flight: September 2, 1947 (P.1040)
Power: Rolls-Royce 2,268kg/5,000lb thrust Nene 101 turbojet
Armament: Four 20mm Hispano cannon beneath cockpit floor
Size: Wingspan – 11.89m/39ft
    Length – 12.08m/39ft 8in
    Height – 2.64m/8ft 8in
    Wing area – 25.83m²/278sq ft
Weights: Empty – 4,173kg/9,200lb
    Maximum take-off – 7,348kg/16,200lb
Performance: Maximum speed – 901kph/560mph
    Ceiling – 13,170m/43,200ft
    Range – 1,191km/740 miles
    Climb – 10,675m/35,000ft in 12 minutes, 5 seconds

LEFT: **Initially known as the FRS.2, the Sea Harrier FA.2 first flew in 1988 and became the Fleet Air Arm's carrier-borne air defence fighter either as new build or converted from the earlier version.**
ABOVE: **The FA.2 was preceded by the FRS.1, an example of which is pictured during the 1982 Falklands War.**

BAE SYSTEMS Harrier/Sea Harrier

The best illustration of British innovation in the field of aircraft design is the Harrier and Sea Harrier. This truly remarkable aircraft, constantly improved and updated since its first hovering flight in October 1960, is still the only single-engined Vertical or Short Take-Off and Landing (V/STOL) in service. It enables military planners to wield air power without the need for airfields.

During the Cold War it was obvious that the West's military airfields would have been attacked very early in any offensive. Dispersal of aircraft and equipment was one response to this – the other was the Harrier with its ability to operate from any small piece of flat ground. The Harrier is equally at home operating from a supermarket car park or woodland clearing as it is from conventional airfields. The fact that a jet plane can fly straight up with no need for forward movement still leaves spectators stunned almost five decades after the prototype carried out its first uncertain and tethered hover.

The Harrier can take off and land vertically by the pilot selecting an 80 degree nozzle angle and applying full power.

ABOVE: **When a mission dictated, the Sea Harrier could have a bolt-on non-retracting inflight refuelling probe fitted.**

At 15–30m/50–100ft altitude, the nozzles are gradually directed rearwards until conventional wingborne flight is achieved. The key to the Harrier's vertical take-off lies with the vectored thrust from the Harrier's Pegasus engine, directed by four jet nozzles controlled by a selector lever next to the throttle in the cockpit. The nozzles swivel as one, directing thrust from directly to the rear to just forward of vertical. While hovering or flying at very low speeds, the aircraft is controlled in all lanes of movement by reaction control jets located in the nose, wing and tail. These jets are operated by the Harrier's conventional rudder pedals and control column.

The Harrier's agility is legendary and it is able to make very tight turns by using the nozzles. In air combat the nozzles can be used to rapidly decelerate the aircraft so that an enemy aircraft, previously on the Harrier's tail, shoots by unable to stop, thus becoming the Harrier's prey instead.

The Harrier GR.1 first entered squadron service with the RAF in October, 1969, and early in the Harrier's operational life, the US Marine Corps expressed an interest in the aircraft, leading to more than 100 being built as the AV-8A by McDonnell Douglas in the US. The other customer for the early Harrier was the Spanish Navy, who ordered the US-built AV-8A and subsequently sold some of the aircraft on to the Thai Navy in 1996.

The Harrier's V/STOL capability was not lost on naval strategists and the Sea Harrier's origins go back to February 1963 when an early version of the Harrier landed on HMS *Ark Royal* at sea. The Royal Navy ordered a maritime version in 1975 and the Sea Harrier FRS. Mk 1 flew for the first time in August, 1978. This aircraft was similar to the Harrier GR.3 but had a completely redesigned front fuselage, different avionics and was powered by a special version of the Pegasus engine (104) with improved corrosion resistance. Examples of this version were exported to the Indian Navy as FRS.51s.

LEFT: **Three stages of Sea Harrier training. The two-seat Hunter (bottom) trained in the use of the Blue Fox radar, while the two-seat Sea Harrier trainer (top) helped pilots transition to the single-seat Sea Harrier.** ABOVE: **Sidewinder-armed FRS.1s.**

The Sea Harrier FA.2 was a mid-life upgrade of the FRS.1 with changes to the airframe, armament, avionics, radar and cockpit. The FA.2 was the first European fighter to be equipped with the AIM-120 AMRAAM air-to-air missile. The Royal Navy's FA.2s made their combat debut in August, 1994, over Bosnia, operated by No.899 Squadron from the deck of HMS *Invincible* but early versions of the Sea Harrier had already been in action with the Fleet Air Arm 12 years earlier. In 1982 Britain's task force sailed south on its 12,872km/8,000-mile journey to retake the Falkland Islands but it faced serious opposition. Against considerable odds, the combined Harrier force of RAF and Fleet Air Arm men and machines flew a total of 1,850 missions and destroyed 32 Argentine aircraft, 23 of them in air combat.

Two-seat trainer versions of all marks of Harrier and Sea Harrier have been produced. In 1998, Britain's Strategic Defence Review proposed Joint Force Harrier (JFH), which called for the management and capabilities of the RN Sea Harrier and RAF Harrier forces to be brought together. In 2001, the decision was taken to decommission the FA.2 Sea Harrier and direct available funding into upgrading the Harrier GR7. Accordingly, on March 28, 2006, a ceremony was held at RNAS Yeovilton to mark the Royal Navy Sea Harrier FA.2's withdrawal from service. In its role as part of JFH, the RAF's Harrier GR7 force remains ready to deploy anywhere in the world, in both sea- and land-based operations.

Serv, 1969 to 2006 37 yr.

ABOVE: **Joint Force Harrier (JFH) RAF aircraft are able to operate from Royal Navy ships at short notice for rapid deployment anywhere the Royal Navy can reach.**

**BAE SYSTEMS
Sea Harrier FA.2**

First flight: September 19, 1988 (FA.2)
Power: Rolls-Royce 9,765kg/21,500lb thrust Pegasus 106 turbofan
Armament: Four AIM-120 air-to-air missiles or two AIM-120s and four AIM-9 Sidewinders; two 30mm Aden cannon can also be carried on underfuselage stations, as well as up to 2,270kg/5,000lb of bombs, rockets and anti-ship missiles
Size: Wingspan – 7.7m/25ft 3in
Length – 14.17m/46ft 6in
Height – 3.71m/12ft 2in
Wing area – 18.7m²/201sq ft
Weights: Empty – 6,374kg/14,052lb
Maximum take-off – 11,880kg/26,200lb
Performance: Maximum speed – 1,185kph/736mph
Ceiling – 15,540m/51,000ft
Range – 1,287km/800 miles
Climb – 15,240m/50,000ft per minute at VTOL weight

Beriev A-40/Be-42 Albatross

The Beriev A-40 and Be-42 (search-and-rescue variant) Albatross, designed to replace the Be-12 and Il-38 in maritime patrol and ASW roles, is the largest amphibious aircraft ever built. Although design work on the Albatross (NATO codename 'Mermaid') began in 1983, it was not known to the West until 1988, when the United States announced that one of their spy satellites had taken photos of a large jet-powered amphibian under development in Russia. The Albatross had, in fact, first flown in December 1986, but its first public appearance was not until Moscow's 1989 Soviet Aviation Day Display. The type entered service in limited numbers in 1990, providing access to remote areas in the east of the former Soviet Union, transporting replacement personnel, carrying out anti-submarine operations and Search-And-Rescue (SAR) missions.

The Albatross is a striking aircraft with high, slightly swept dihedral wings and slender fuselage, while booster jet engines are faired in beneath the two main large turbofan engines placed over the wing. Floats are attached at the very end of the wings by short pylons, while the large inflight refuelling probe atop the nose and the high 'T' tail are also key features. The

TOP: **This excellent head-on study of the A-40 shows the engines set high and towards the rear of the wing to protect them from water ingestion. This example has its undercarriage deployed and is taxiing on to dry land.** ABOVE: **Note the rudder at the base of the tail for water taxiing, and the large refuelling probe on the top of the nose.**

take-off run for this vast aircraft is 1,000m/3,281ft on land and 2,000m/6,562ft on water while the landing run on land is 700m/2,297ft and 900m/2,953ft on water. The aircraft had a standard crew of eight consisting of two pilots, a flight engineer, radio operator, navigator and three observers.

The type's ability to land in 2m/6ft swells led to the development of the Be-42 SAR version, designed to take up to 54 survivors of an incident at sea. Equipment included life-rafts, powerboats and a range of specialist medical equipment while the aircraft was also equipped with infrared sensors and a searchlight to find victims in the water.

The Albatross secured over 140 performance records very early in its

ABOVE: **The smaller Be-200 was derived from the A-40 and retained the same high tail and high-set engine configuration as the Albatross.**

1986 testing flights – for example, it had the ability to lift 10 tons of cargo to 3,000m/9,843ft in just 3 minutes. Despite

this, the type has only been produced in small numbers to date because it was entering production as the former Soviet Union was collapsing.

Nervertheless, the aircraft represented a potent anti-submarine weapon system. It can fly far out to sea, perhaps 2,000km/1,250 miles, at high speed, find and attack an enemy sub using depth charges, then land on the water to listen for the enemy craft using a barrage of electronic aids and sensors. The aircraft's endurance and inflight refuelling ability meant it could track a target for days.

The Beriev Be-200, derived from the A-40, is a smaller twin-engine amphibious aircraft available in transport, passenger-carrying, fire-fighting, patrol and search-and-rescue versions. South Korea has expressed interest in a maritime patrol version of this Albatross derivative.

TOP: **The first prototype. Note the aircraft's distinctive planing bottom, very large radome and very long trailing-edge flaps.** ABOVE: **Coming in to land. Note the location of the extended undercarriage, the split rudder and the all-moving tailplane.** BELOW LEFT: **The fillet just forward of the fin housed the aircraft's self-defence chaff and flare dispensers. The port main engine is positioned immediately above the port booster jet.**

Beriev A-40

First flight: December 1986
Power: Two Aviadvigatel 12,016kg/26,455lb thrust D-30KPV turbofans and two RKBM 2,502kg/5,510lb thrust RD-60K booster turbojets
Armament: 6,500kg/14,330lb of bombs, torpedoes or mines carried in internal weapons bay
Size: Wingspan – 41.62m/136ft 7in
   Length – 38.92m/127ft 8in
   Height – 11.07m/36ft 4in
   Wing area – 200m^2/2,152sq ft
Weights: Maximum take-off – 86,000kg/189,595lb
Performance: Maximum speed – 760kph/472mph
   Ceiling – 9,706m/31,825ft
   Range – 5,500km/3,416 miles
   Climb – 915m/3,000ft per minute

Beriev Be-12

The amphibious twin-engine Beriev Be-12 (NATO codename 'Mail') was one of two large flying boats, previously unknown to the West, that first appeared at Moscow's Soviet Aviation Day flypast of 1961. While Beriev's swept-wing, jet-powered Be-10 attracted a great deal of attention, the turboprop-powered Be-12 drew little. Western analysts believed it to be a one-off experimental turboprop version of the earlier piston-powered Be-6 that first flew in 1949. The Be-12 was in fact a replacement for the Be-6 although it shared the earlier type's twin tails and gull wing – this latter feature led to its name of 'Tchaika' (Seagull) and was necessary to keep the engines and propellers as far as possible from the damaging waves and salt water. The Be-12 went on to become the standard equipment of the Soviet coastal anti-submarine force, entering service in 1964, while the Be-10 was never seen in public again. Over four decades on, the Be-12 was

ABOVE: **In addition to its military roles the Be-12 has been developed for a number of other uses including water bombing. Two aircraft were converted to the fire-bomber role, designated Be-12P (*Protivopozarnyi* – Fire protection).**

still in service around Russia's coasts, and had earned a reputation for being tough and versatile.

In the late 1950s, the US began development of the first generation Polaris nuclear-missile submarines. Due to the missile's range and accuracy limitations, the launch submarine had to be fairly close to the target country's coastline. In response to this threat, the AV-MF (*Aviatsiya Voenno-Morskovo Flota* – Soviet Naval Air Force) issued a 1956 requirement for an aircraft that could detect and kill enemy nuclear-missile submarines in USSR coastal waters.

The aircraft was developed on the assumption that any threat would first be picked up by shipborne or land-based detection systems and give the search aircraft a fairly accurate location which would then be thoroughly scrutinized by the aircraft's short-range radar, Magnetic Anomaly Detection (MAD) probe and sonobouys. An attack against a 'bogey' would then

LEFT: **An excellent study of a Be-12 showing the distinctive glazed nose, the start of the planing bottom and the large radome.** ABOVE: **A classic Cold War photo taken from a NATO aircraft. If the Cold War had heated up, the Be-12 would have played a key role in reducing the threat from enemy Polaris submarines.**

take place, usually in co-operation with surface ships. In contrast, by this time, Western naval air forces were starting to phase out flying boats for maritime patrol duties and were instead turning to long-range landplane types such as the Avro Shackleton and Lockheed P-3 Orion. Soviet plans for high-performance amphibian aircraft in this role had to be shelved when the Be-10 was found to have been built for performance and not its military capability. The Be-10 was cancelled and Tupolev Tu-16 'Badger' bombers were instead adapted for the naval role. However, the Be-12 was retained as its capabilities offered the Soviets true flexibility when policing their home waters.

Be-12s were developed with a weapons bay in the rear hull, as well as external wing pylons for carrying ordnance. Although the first prototype retained the retractable 'dustbin' search radar used on the Be-6, later aircraft had a prominent nose search radar in place of the 'dustbin'. With long endurance and the ability to take over many other roles, the Be-12 was approved for AV-MF service.

Production started in 1963 and continued for a decade during which time 143 aircraft, including development machines, were built. The Be-12 officially entered service with the AV-MF in spring 1964 with the primary role of ASW patrol, operating some 500km/310 miles from shore. By 1967 the Be-12 had replaced the Be-6 entirely for front-line duties and then was used for other duties including coastal surveillance, multi-sensor reconnaissance, anti-shipping patrol, photographic survey, naval co-operation, transport, and search-and-rescue. Over the years, the Be-12 has gained no fewer than 44 aviation world records for its class for time to altitude, speed and payload.

In military service the Be-12's avionics and surveillance was upgraded a number of times to maintain its viability in dealing with the ever-evolving Cold War threat from the West. From 1970, as the US Polaris submarines evolved and could launch

ABOVE: **This photograph shows many of the Be-12s distinguishing features, including the inverted gull wing, twin-fin tailplane and hull.** BELOW: **The name 'Tchaika' (Seagull) came from the aircraft's wing configuration, which allowed engines and propellers to remain far from the water surface, minimizing the danger of water ingestion damage and corrosion. The body of the aircraft housed a weapons bay aft of the hull step.**

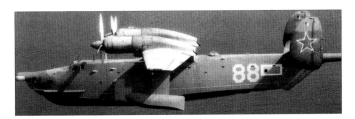

from a much greater distance, the coastal ASW patrol role of the Be-12 declined and the type took on more secondary roles. In 1972, some were converted for the high-speed Search and Rescue role, designated Be-12PS. Other roles included fishery protection, transport, mapping and survey, and whaling patrol.

During its career, the Be-12 served with all four of the Soviet Fleet's Naval Aviation forces – Pacific, Northern, Black Sea and Baltic – equipping up to 12 squadrons of 8 aircraft each, as well as a number of independent squadrons. By 2005, the Russian Navy were still operating only 12 Be-12s, but the type is expected to fly on for the foreseeable future.

ABOVE: **Other weapons can be carried on four underwing pylons. The front radome holds a search radar, integrated with a rear-mounted MAD that searched for submarines. The aircraft had a crew of five.**

Beriev Be-12

First flight: October 18, 1960 (prototype)

Power: Two 5,180shp ZMDB Progress AI-20DK turboprop engines

Armament: Up to 3,000kg/6,614lb of depth charges and sonobuoys in internal weapons bay plus mines, bombs, anti-shipping missiles, torpedoes or rockets on underwing hard points

Size: Wingspan – 29.84m/97ft 11in
Length – 30.11m/98ft 9in
Height – 7.94m/26ft 1in
Wing area – 99m^2/1,065sq ft

Weights: Empty – 24,000kg/52,910lb
Maximum take-off – 29,500kg/65,040lb

Performance: Maximum speed – 530kph/330mph
Ceiling – 8,000m/26,250ft
Range – 3,300km/2,051 miles
Climb – 912m/2,990ft per minute

LEFT: **An RAF Buccaneer S.2 with its Gulf War nose art. The last RAF front-line Buccaneers were retired in March 1994.** ABOVE: **The Royal Aircraft Establishment at Farnborough operated a number of 'Buccs' as trials aircraft in this distinctive 'raspberry ripple' paint scheme.** BELOW: **This Buccaneer S.2B was one of the Fleet Air Arm aircraft that passed into Royal Air Force use. Note the catapult launch strop falling away from the aircraft. Strop catchers were introduced on HMS *Ark Royal*'s catapults to retrieve the strops for re-use.**

Blackburn Buccaneer

The Buccaneer was the last all-British bomber aircraft design and, in its day, it was the most advanced high-speed low-level strike aircraft in the world. It had its origins in the July 1953 Naval Staff requirement N.A.39, which called for a long-range carrier-borne transonic strike aircraft capable of carrying a nuclear weapon beneath enemy radar cover and attacking enemy shipping or ports.

Blackburn's N.A.39 response, the B-103, was the successful contender and the development contract was awarded in 1955 – the first of 20 pre-production aircraft took to the air on April 30, 1958, and also appeared at that year's Farnborough air show. The B-103 prototype was powered by 3,175kg/7,000lb thrust Gyron turbojets, not the much more powerful Spey of later models. The carrier aircraft elements of the design, such as folding wings, folding nose catapult fittings and arrester hook, were introduced from the fourth aircraft onwards.

The aerodynamically advanced aircraft incorporated many innovations, including a rotary bomb bay door (intended to avoid the drag of conventional bomb bay doors and weapons carried beneath the aircraft) and a vertically-split tail cone which opened to act as airbrakes. The aircraft also had a cutting-edge boundary layer control system in which air from the engines was forced through slits on the wings' leading edges, producing much more lift than that wing would normally give. Increasing the wings' efficiency meant the aircraft could land at lower speed and carry more ordnance – perfect for carrier operations.

The Miniature Detonating Cord (MDC), now standard on most British fast jets, which shatters the cockpit canopy prior to ejection, was pioneered on this Blackburn design. It was actually developed to aid escape in the event of underwater ejection.

Royal Navy carrier trials began in January 1960, and the first B-103 deck landing took place on HMS *Victorious* on the 19th

of the month. Having given the aircraft the name Buccaneer in 1960, the Navy took delivery of the first production version, the S.1, in July 1962. HMS *Ark Royal* sailed with the first operational Buccaneer squadron, No.801, and its anti-flash white (for protection against the nuclear flash of the weapons it used) Buccaneers only six months later in January 1963. The Cold War was at one of its chilliest phases and Britain wanted nuclear-capable aircraft in service as soon as possible.

The S.1 was soon shown to be under-powered and in some conditions the Gyrons could barely lift a loaded Buccaneer off the deck within safety margins. Consequently, Fleet Air Arm Scimitars fitted with inflight refuelling equipment were detailed to refuel the partly fuelled and therefore lighter Buccaneers shortly after they left the deck. Forty S.1s were built before production switched to the next mark. The improved S.2 was the principal production version (84 built) and had a greater range than the earlier version thanks to the more powerful but less thirsty Spey engines. Service S.2s are most easily recognized by the fixed refuelling probe on the nose forward of the cockpit. A retractable refuelling probe proved problematic so instead a fixed probe was introduced, marring the Buccaneer's otherwise clean lines.

The S.2s served in the Royal Navy's front line from January 1967 until the last S.2s left the deck of the *Ark Royal* in November 1978. The Buccaneer's career was, however, far from over as the first of almost 90 aircraft had begun service with the Royal Air Force in October 1969, filling the gap in the RAF inventory left by the scrapping of TSR.2 and the cancellation of the intended F-111 purchase for the RAF. Of the RAF Buccaneers, 26 were new-build, while a further 62 Royal Navy examples were gradually transferred into RAF service. As well as retaining a nuclear strike capability, Buccaneers were also tasked with anti-shipping missions from land bases. RAF Germany, right in the nuclear front line, first welcomed No.15 Squadron's Buccaneers early in 1971. Tornados began to replace the Germany Buccaneers in 1983, but two squadrons tasked with maritime strike remained in service in Scotland. In 1991 some of these aircraft were 'called up' for service in the first Gulf War, where they acted as laser designators for laser-guided bombs dropped by Tornados. To give it even longer range for these special missions, the 'Bucc' was fitted with a 2000-litre/440-gallon fuel tank carried in the bomb bay.

TOP: **The Buccaneer gave the Royal Navy a powerful nuclear punch during some of the most tense years of the Cold War. Note the fixed refuelling probe on these FAA S.2s.** ABOVE: **The Buccaneer's wings were hinged to fold up to 120 degrees.** BELOW: **A Buccaneer S.1, arrester hook deployed, prepares to catch the wire. The paint scheme is extra-dark sea grey on the upper surfaces and anti-flash gloss white on the undersides. Note the tail airbrakes.**

Blackburn Buccaneer S.2

First flight: April 30, 1958 (B-103 prototype)
Power: Two Rolls-Royce 5,035kg/11,100lb thrust Rolls-Royce Spey 101 turbofans
Armament: One nuclear bomb or four 454kg/1,000lb conventional bombs carried internally
Size: Wingspan – 13.41m/44ft
Length – 19.33m/63ft 5in
Height – 4.95m/16ft 3in
Wing area – 47.82m²/515sq ft
Weights: Empty –13,608kg/30,000lb
Maximum take-off – 28,123kg/62,000lb
Performance: Maximum speed – 1,038kph/645mph
Ceiling – 12,190m/40,000ft plus
Range – 3,700km/2,300 miles
Climb – 9,144m/30,000ft in 2 minutes

LEFT: **A heavily laden F/A-18 of VMFA-323 Marine Fighter Attack Squadron 323. Note the large centreline auxiliary fuel tank.** ABOVE: **The F/A-18 pilot has one of the world's most versatile and high-performance military aircraft under his or her control. Note the excellent all-round visibility from the 'bubble' cockpit.**

Boeing/McDonnell Douglas/ Northrop F/A-18 Hornet

The Hornet, today's premier naval fighter, was developed for the US Navy from the YF-17 project proposed for the US Air Force by Northrop. As the company had no experience building carrier-borne aircraft, it teamed up with McDonnell Douglas (now Boeing) to offer a developed F-17. Initially two versions – ground attack and fighter – were proposed, but the two roles were combined in the very capable F/A-18, the first of which flew in 1978. Among the Hornet's features are fly-by-wire, folding wingtips and an advanced cockpit including head-up display and Hands-On Throttle And Stick (HOTAS).

With its excellent fighter and self-defence capabilities, the F/A-18 was intended to increase strike mission survivability and supplement the F-14 Tomcat in US Navy fleet air defence. The F/A-18 played a key role in the 1986 US strikes against Libya. Flying from the USS *Coral Sea*, F/A-18s launched High-speed Anti-Radiation Missiles (HARMs) against Libyan air defence radars and missile sites, thus silencing them during the attacks on military targets in Benghazi.

The F/A-18's advanced radar and avionics systems allow Hornet pilots to shift from fighter to strike mode on the same mission with the flip of a switch, a facility used routinely by Hornets in Operation 'Desert Storm' – they fought their way to a target by defeating opposing aircraft, attacked ground targets and returned safely home. This 'force multiplier' capability gives the operational commander more flexibility in employing tactical aircraft in a rapidly changing battle scenario.

The F/A-18 Hornet was built in single- and two-seat versions. Although the two-seater is a conversion trainer, it is combat-capable and has a similar performance to the single-seat version although with reduced range. The F/A-18A and C are single-seat aircraft while the F/A-18B and D are dual-seaters. The B model is used primarily for training, while the D model is the current US Navy aircraft for attack, tactical air control, forward air control and reconnaissance squadrons.

The improved F/A-18C first flew in 1986 and featured improved avionics, AIM-120 and AGM-65 compatibility and a new central computer.

ABOVE: **The carrier USS *John C. Stennis* embarked Air Wing operates the F/A-18 Hornet, F/A-18E/F Super Hornet, EA-6B Prowler, E-2C Hawkeye and MH-60S Seahawk.**

LEFT: **A missile-armed Hornet of US Navy Attack Squadron 82 (VA-82), operating from the carrier USS *America*. Note the missile carried on the wingtip.**
ABOVE: **An F/A-18C of US Navy Strike Fighter Squadron 86 (VFA-86), the 'Sidewinders', prepares to launch from the deck of USS *Enterprise* (CVN-65) in the Arabian Gulf. This is the eighth US naval vessel to bear the name.**

In November 1989, the first F/A-18s equipped with night-strike capability were delivered to the US Navy, and since 1991, F/A-18s have been delivered with F404-GE-402 enhanced performance engines that produce up to 20 per cent more thrust than the previous F404 engines. From May 1994, the Hornet has been equipped with upgraded radar – the APG-73 – which substantially increases the speed and memory capacity of the radar's processors. These upgrades and improvements help the Hornet maintain its advantage over potential enemies and keep it among the most advanced and capable combat aircraft in the world, not just naval types.

Apart from the US Navy and Marine Corps, the F/A-18 is also in service with the air forces of Canada, Australia, Spain, Kuwait, Finland, Switzerland and Malaysia.

Canada was the first international customer for the F/A-18, and its fleet of 138 CF-18 Hornets is the largest outside the United States. The CF-18s have an unusual element to their paint scheme in that a 'fake' cockpit is painted on the underside of the fuselage directly beneath the real cockpit. This is intended to confuse an enemy fighter, if only for a split second, about the orientation of the CF-18 in close air combat. That moment's hesitation can mean the difference between kill or be killed in a dogfight situation.

Current plans say that F-18A/B aircraft will remain in service with the United States Navy until about 2015 while F-18C/D models will be retired by 2020.

ABOVE: **Two F/A-18s of the US Marine Corps. The aircraft in the foreground is the two-seat combat–capable F/A-18D trainer flying alongside a single-seat F/A-18C.**

Boeing/McDonnell Douglas/Northrop F/A-18C Hornet

First flight: November 17, 1978
Power: Two General Electric 7,721kg/17,000lb thrust afterburning F404-GE-402 turbofans
Armament: One 20mm cannon and up to 7,031kg/15,500lb of weapons, including AIM-120 AMRAAM, AIM-7, AIM-9 air-to-air missiles or other guided weapons such as rockets and tactical nuclear weapons
Size: Wingspan – 11.43m/37ft 6in
Length – 17.07m/56ft
Height – 4.66m/15ft 3.5in
Wing area – 37.16m^2/400sq ft
Weights: Empty – 10,455kg/23,050lb
Maximum take-off – 25,401kg/56,000lb
Performance: Maximum speed – 1,915kph/1,189mph
Ceiling – 15,240m/50,000ft plus
Combat radius – 1,020km/634 miles
Climb – 13,715m/45,000ft per minute

Boeing/McDonnell Douglas/ Northrop F/A-18E Super Hornet

The combat-proven F/A-18E/F Super Hornet is the most capable multi-role strike fighter available today or for the foreseeable future. In the words of its manufacturers, "The Super Hornet is an adverse-weather, day and night, multi-mission strike fighter whose survivability improvements over its predecessors make it harder to find, and if found, harder to hit, and if hit, harder to disable."

TOP: **The Super Hornet successfully conducted its initial carrier trials aboard the carrier USS** *John C. Stennis* **(CVN-74) in January 1997. By April 1999, trails aircraft had conducted 7,700 hours of tests.** ABOVE: **A two-seat F/A-18F equipped for 'buddy' refuelling tops up an F/A-18 E.**

The F/A-18E/F Super Hornet was devised to build on the great success of the Hornet and having been test flown in November 1995, entered service for evaluation with US Navy squadron VFA-122 in November 1999. The Super Hornet was developed by a team including Boeing, Northrop Grumman, GE Aircraft Engines, Raytheon and more than 1,800 suppliers in the United States and Canada.

The first production model was delivered to the US Navy in December 1998, more than a month ahead of schedule and – after completing the most thorough operational evaluation in US Naval history – the F/A-18E/F Super Hornet entered operational service in November 1999. The first operational cruise of the F/A-18 E Super Hornet was with VFA-115 on board the USS *Abraham Lincoln* (CVN-72) on July 24, 2002, and the type was first used in combat on November 6, 2002, when they participated in a strike on hostile targets – two surface-to-air missile launchers and an air-defence command-and-control bunker in the 'no-fly' zone in Iraq. One of the pilots, Lt John Turner, dropped 907kg/2000lb JDAM bombs for the first time from the F/A-18E in wartime. VFA-115 embarked aboard *Lincoln* expended twice the amount of

bombs as other squadrons in their air wing (with 100 per cent accuracy) and met and exceeded all readiness requirements while on deployment. On September 8, 2006, VFA-211 F/A-18F Super Hornets expended GBU-12 and GBU-38 bombs against Taliban fighters and fortifications west and north-west of Kandahar – the first time the unit had gone into combat with the Super Hornet.

Since its inception, the Super Hornet programme has remained on time, on weight and on cost. In 1999, to acknowledge this acheivement, the F/A-18 programme team was awarded the prestigious Collier Trophy. The award recognizes the greatest achievement in aeronautics and astronautics in the United States, and has been called the greatest and most prized of all aeronautical honours in the United States.

The Super Hornet is 25 per cent larger than its predecessor but has 42 per cent fewer parts. Both the single-seat E and two-seat F models offer increased range, greater endurance, more payload-carrying ability and more powerful engines in the form of two F414-GE-400s, an advanced derivative of the Hornet's current F404 engine family that produces 35 per cent more thrust, a combined 19,960kg/44,000lb. The F414's light yet robust design yields a 9:1 thrust-to-weight ratio, one of the highest of any modern fighter engine. Increased airflow to the engine is provided through the Super Hornet's large, distinctively shaped inlets. A full authority digital electronics control (FADEC) allows for unrestricted engine response in any phase of flight.

Structural changes to the airframe increase internal fuel capacity by 1,633kg/3,600lb, which extends the Hornet's mission radius by up to 40 per cent. The fuselage is 86.3cm/34in longer and the wing is 25 per cent larger with an extra 9.3m^2/100sq ft of surface area.

There are 2 additional weapons stations, bringing the total to 11 and bestowing considerable payload flexibility by carrying a mixed load of air-to-air and air-to-ground ordnance. A typical basic load out for a self-escort strike mission starts with an advanced infrared targeting pod, one AIM-120 AMRAAM, two AIM-9 Sidewinder missiles, and an external fuel tank. This leaves six underwing weapon stations available to carry a variety of weapons and other stores.

Two versions of the Super Hornet – the single-seat E model and the two-seat F model – are in production today and in service with the US Navy. Both are true multi-role aircraft, able to perform virtually every mission in the tactical spectrum including air superiority, day/night strike with precision-guided weapons, fighter escort, close air support, suppression of enemy air defence, maritime strike, reconnaissance, forward air control and tanker duties.

The F/A-18E/F has exceptional combat manoeuvrability, an unlimited angle of attack, high resistance to spins, and ease of handling and training. Its reconfigurable digital flight control system can detect damage to or full loss of a flight control and still allow safe recovery. These and other enhancements will ensure that the Super Hornet remains combat relevant well into the 21st century.

TOP: **The F/A-18E is 25 per cent larger than the Hornet and has 11 weapon-carrying stations. Note the variety of munitions carried and the empty pylons.**
ABOVE: **Armourers prepare to load a GBU-12, a 227kg/500lb laser-guided weapon on an F/A-18E.** ABOVE RIGHT: **An F/A-18F goes vertical with a full missile load. The aircraft is from Strike Fighter Squadron 122 (VFA-122), also known as the 'Flying Eagles', a United States Navy F/A-18E/F Super Hornet training or fleet replacement squadron.**

BELOW: **An F/A-18E leaves the carrier deck – note the green 'go' light visible in the bottom left of the photo.**

Boeing/McDonnell Douglas/Northrop F/A-18E Super Hornet

First flight: November 18, 1995
Power: Two General Electric 9,992kg/22,000lb thrust afterburning F414-GE-400 turbofans
Armament: One 20mm cannon, 11 hardpoints carrying up to 8,050kg/17,750lb of weapons including AIM-7, AIM-120 AMRAAM, AIM-9 air-to-air missiles or other guided weapons, bombs and rockets
Size: Wingspan – 13.62m/44ft 9in
Length – 18.31m/60ft 1in
Height – 4.88m/16ft
Wing area – 46.5m^2/500sq ft
Weights: Empty – 13,410kg/29,574lb
Maximum take-off – 29,937/66,000lb
Performance: Maximum speed – 1,915kph/1,189mph
Ceiling – 15,240m/50,000ft plus
Combat radius – 2,225km/1,382 miles

LEFT: **The Breguet Alizé was flying in front-line service over four decades after the prototype first took to the air.** ABOVE: **Wings folded but being prepared for flight, these two examples are pictured on the deck of a French aircraft carrier. Note the weapons hardpoints on the underside of the folded wing on the aircraft shown at the top.**

Breguet Alizé

The carrier-borne anti-submarine Alizé (tradewind) was derived from the Vultur carrier-based strike aircraft that was designed for the French Aéronavale but never produced for service. The Alizé was an extensive redesign of the earlier type and was developed for the anti-submarine role – it had its first flight on October 6, 1956. A low-wing monoplane of conventional configuration, the Alizé carried a radar system with a retractable 'dustbin' radome installed in the belly. The type had a tricycle undercarriage and the main landing gear retracted backwards into nacelles beneath the wings which folded hydraulically. The first production machine was handed over to the French Navy on May 29, 1959.

The cockpit accommodated a crew of three consisting of a pilot seated in front on the right, radar operator in front on the left and the sensor operator sat sideways behind them. The internal weapons bay could accommodate a homing torpedo or depth charges, and underwing stores pylons could carry bombs, depth charges, rockets or missiles. Typical underwing stores included 68mm rocket pods or AS.12 wire-guided anti-ship missiles. The Alizé, powered by the Rolls-Royce Dart RDa.21 turboprop driving a four-bladed propeller, could patrol for over five hours and cover vast areas of ocean thereby providing a valuable defence for French naval assets.

A total of 89 examples of the Alizé were built between 1957 and 1962, including prototypes. The Aéronavale operated 75 from March 1959 on board the carriers *Clemenceau* and *Foch*.

The Aéronavale provided the Alizé with a series of upgrades to ensure the aircraft was able to meet the ever-changing challenges of naval warfare. An early 1980s modernization programme upgraded 28 of the aircraft to Br.1050M standard by the introduction of the Thomson-CSF Iguane radar (as used on Breguet's Atlantique maritime reconnaissance aircraft), new OMEGA radio navigation, and a new ARAR 12 radar and radio location system. Another upgrade programme in the early 1990s fitted 24 of these aircraft with, among other refinements, a new decoy system and a computer-based data-processing system. Later in the 1990s, they were fitted with the Thomson-CSF TTD Optronique Chlio Forward-Looking Infra-Red (FLIR) imaging sensor system.

The Alizé was used in combat during the 1999 NATO air campaign against Serbian forces over Kosovo in the spring of 1999, with the aircraft flying off the French carrier *Foch*.

The last Breguet Alizé was withdrawn from front-line service in 2000 with the retirement of the *Foch*. Despite the many upgrades, by this

ABOVE: **This aircraft, 04, was the first of two pre-production machines built after the three prototypes. It first flew on June 21, 1957, and was used to develop operational procedures and is shown during deck trials at sea.**

time the Alizé was clearly not up to the task of hunting modern nuclear submarines.

The Indian Navy operated the Alizé (around 20 examples) from shorebases and from the light carrier *Vikrant*. The type was used for reconnaissance and patrol during India's 1961 occupation of Portuguese Goa, and was also used for anti-submarine patrol during the Indo-Pakistan War of 1971, during which one Alizé was shot down by a Pakistani F-104 Starfighter in what must have been a most unusual air-combat episode. Numerous Pakistani gunboats were also destroyed by the Alizé in the conflict.

Indian Alizés were gradually relegated to shore-based patrol duties in the 1980s, and were finally phased out in 1992. Like the British Fairey Gannet which they so resembled, the Alizés were replaced by ASW helicopters.

ABOVE: **Aircraft prepare to launch from a French aircraft carrier. The Alizé did not have to use catapults to get airborne, but could just use the whole length of the carrier's deck.** BELOW: **A typical Alizé mission would last for 4 hours, during which the aircraft would consume 2,000 litres/440 gallons of fuel. It would then undergo 30 hours of maintenance to prepare for the next mission.**

ABOVE: **Note the yoke-type arrester hook as this aircraft prepares to land. To help prevent salt-water corrosion each aircraft was thoroughly washed every three weeks while at sea.**

Breguet Alizé

First flight: October 5, 1956 (prototype)

Power: One Rolls-Royce 1,975hp Dart RDa.21 turboprop

Armament: Acoustic torpedo, three 160kg/353lb depth charges housed in internal bomb bay; two anti-shipping missiles carried beneath the folding wings, or a combination of depth charges, bombs or rockets

Size: Wingspan – 15.6m/51ft 2in

Length – 13.86m/45ft 6in

Height – 5m/16ft 4.75in

Wing area – 36m²/388sq ft

Weights: Empty – 5,700kg/12,566lb

Maximum take-off – 8,200kg/18,078lb

Performance: Maximum speed – 518kph/322mph

Ceiling – 8,000m/26,245ft plus

Range – 2,500km/1,553 miles

Climb – 420m/1,380ft per minute

Dassault Etendard and Super Etendard

Dassault speculatively developed their Etendard (Standard) design to meet the needs of both French national and NATO programmes for new light fighters reflecting the air combat experiences of the Korean War. Various versions did not get beyond the prototype stage but then the Etendard IV multi-role carrier-based fighter drew the attention of the French Navy who for a time had considered the navalized SEPECAT Jaguar for the role. This led to the development of the Etendard IV M specifically for the French Navy – it was the first naval aircraft developed by Dassault.

The Etendard IV M made its maiden flight in May 1958, and from 1961 until 1965 the French Navy took delivery of 69 Etendard IV Ms that served on the French carriers *Foch* and *Clemenceau* – 21 reconnaissance/tanker versions designated Etendard IV Ps also served. The Etendard IV M continued to serve in the French Navy until July 1991 by which time they had logged 180,000 flying hours and made 25,300 carrier landings.

The search for an Etendard replacement led to Dassault proposing the Super Etendard, an updated and much improved aircraft, based on the Etendard IV M but 90 per cent a new design. Designed both for strike and interception duties, it featured the more powerful Atar 8K-50 engine and a strengthened structure to withstand higher speed operations. The weapons system was improved through the installation of a modern navigation and combat management system centered on a Thomson multi-mode radar. The wing had a new leading edge and revised flaps which, with the newer engine, eased the take-off of the heavier Super Etendard.

The Super Etendard prototype made its maiden flight on October 28, 1974, and the first of 71 production aircraft were delivered from mid-1978, again for service on the aircraft carriers *Foch* and *Clemenceau*. One hundred Super Etendards were planned for the Navy but spiraling costs called for a reduction of the order.

ABOVE: **The Etendard IV P reconnaissance version had a fixed refuelling probe and cameras in the nose. Note the arrester hook beneath the tail. The 'blade' aerial under the nose was used to guide the AS.30 missiles launched by the aircraft.**
LEFT: **The Etendard prototype first flew in July 1956 and was designed with the latest knowledge of aerodynamics, including 'area' rule.**
INSET: **The all-French Super Etendard won out as an Etendard replacement over the more advanced Jaguar M which was half British.**

LEFT: **French naval air power, both bought-in and homegrown. Aéronavale Super Etendards and F-8 Crusaders pictured over the French Navy aircraft carrier *Clemenceau*. Note the long length of the Super Etendard's noseleg.**

Armed with two 30mm cannon, the Super Etendard could carry a variety of weaponry on its five hardpoints including two Matra Magic AAMs, four pods of 18 68mm rockets, a variety of bombs or two Exocet anti-ship missiles. A number were also modified to carry the Aérospatiale ASMP stand-off nuclear bomb.

The Argentine Navy's use of the Super Etendard/Exocet combination during the Falklands War of 1982 proved devastating against British ships – Argentina had ordered fourteen Super Etendards from Dassault in 1979 but only five aircraft and reportedly five missiles had been delivered by the time France embargoed arms shipments to Argentina. These five strike fighters, with pilots unwilling to engage the agile British Harriers in air combat, nevertheless proved to be a very potent element of the Argentine inventory.

On May 4, 1982, two Super Etendards took off from a base in Argentina preparing to attack the British task force. After three hours and an inflight refuelling, the aircraft located and launched an attack on the British ships. One of the Exocets

found and severely damaged the frigate HMS *Sheffield* which sank on May 10. On May 25, two Exocet-equipped Super Etendards again attacked the task force, this time sinking the *Atlantic Conveyor* with its cargo of nine helicopters.

A handful of Super Etendards were supplied to Iraq in October, 1983 as the Iraqis were desperate to cripple Iran by attacking tankers in the Persian Gulf with Exocets. Around 50 ships were attacked in the Gulf in 1984, the majority of the actions apparently carried out by Iraqi Super Etendards.

Production ended in 1983 but the Super Etendards underwent continuous modernization through the 1990s to enable them to use the latest laser-guided 'smart' weapons. These updated aircraft, designated Super Etendard Modernisé (SEM), participated in NATO's 1999 operations over Kosovo as well as strike missions over Afghanistan as part of Operation 'Enduring Freedom'.

All remaining Super Etendards are expected to be retired from French service by 2010, their replacement by naval Rafale Ms having begun in 2006.

LEFT: **The Dassault Etendard gave great service to the French Navy for a number of years. Note that only the Etendard wingtips folded since swept wings take up less room on carrier decks.**

Dassault Super Etendard

First flight: October 28, 1974

Power: SNECMA 5,000kg/11,025lb afterburning thrust Atar 8K-50 turbojet

Armament: Two 30mm cannon, plus 2,100kg/4,630lb of weapons including Matra Magic AAMs, AM39 Exocet ASMs, bombs and rockets

Size: Wingspan – 9.6m/31ft 6in
Length – 14.31m/46ft 11.5in
Height – 3.86m/12ft 8in
Wing area – 28.4m^2/306sq ft

Weights: Empty – 6,500kg/14,330lb
Maximum take-off – 12,000kg/26,455lb

Performance: Maximum speed – 1,205kph/749mph
Ceiling – 13,700m/44,950ft
Range – 650km/404 miles
Climb – 6,000m/19,685ft per minute

RIGHT: **Dassault built 75 Etendard IVMs and 22 IVPs. Three IVMs were converted to Super Etendard standard to test and prove the design.**

LEFT: **A French Navy Rafale M from the French carrier *Charles De Gaulle* performs a touch-and-go landing aboard the USS *Dwight D. Eisenhower* (CVN-69), during the Multi-National Maritime Exercise in May 2005.** ABOVE: **Described by its manufacturers as "omnirole by design", the Rafale was a purely French design and was "provided with distinctive features tuned to worldwide – opposed to strictly West European – market expectations".**

Dassault Rafale

Even as the Mirage 2000 was entering French Air Force service in the early 1980s, a successor was already being sought to be the prime French Air Force fighter. After France withdrew from what became the Eurofighter programme, attention was then focused on Dassault's *Avion de Combat Experimentale* (ACX), which first flew on July 4, 1986, and was later designated Rafale A. This demonstrator aircraft was used to test the basic design including the airframe, powerplant and the fly-by-wire system.

Directly derived from the slightly larger (3 per cent) Rafale A demonstrator, production Rafales appear in three versions – the single-seat air-defence Rafale C (for *chasseur*), the two-seater trainer/multi-role Rafale B (*biplace*) and the single-seat Rafale M (*marine*) fighter for the Navy. The three versions are fitted with the same engines (the SNECMA M88-2), navigation/attack system, aircraft-management system and flight-control systems. The cockpit has Hands-On Throttle and Stick (HOTAS) controls, a wide-angle head-up display, two Multi-Function Display (MFD) monitors showing all flight and instrument information, and a helmet-mounted weapons sight. Voice recognition is planned to feature in future versions

so the pilot will be able to issue orders to the aircraft simply by using his or her voice – even in the early 21st century this is a remarkable proposition.

All three versions have the same 213kph/132mph approach speed and a take-off/landing run of less than 400m/1312ft, made possible by complimenting the delta wing with canard foreplanes which together optimize aerodynamic efficiency and stability control without impeding the pilot's visibility. The materials employed and the shapes that make up the aircraft have both been carefully selected to minimize the aircraft's electro-magnetic and infrared signature to make it as 'stealthy' as possible. Carbon and Kevlar composites, superplastic-formed diffusion-bonded titanium and aluminium-lithium alloys have all been used in this aircraft.

The first production aircraft, Rafale B1, flew in December 1998 while the single-seat Rafale C, an air defence fighter with fully integrated weapons and navigation systems, had its first flight on May 19, 1991. Making full use of the latest technology, it is capable of outstanding performance on multiple air-to-air targets.

The two-seat multi-role Rafale B first took to the air on April 30, 1993, and retains most of the elements of the single-seater version, and its weapon and navigation system is exactly the same. The Rafale B can undertake an operational mission with just a pilot as crew or with a pilot and a weapons system operator. In Armée de l'Air service, the B model was chosen to replace the popular ground-attack Jaguar, and can carry up to 8,000kg/17,600lb of weaponry – in the air-to-air role this includes up to eight Matra Mica AAM missiles.

LEFT: **The Rafale's delta wing and close-coupled canards ensure a wide range of centre of gravity positions for all flight conditions, as well as benign handling throughout the flight envelope.**

The Rafale M was ordered to replace the French Navy's ageing fleet of F-8 Crusaders, and is a single-seat fighter modified for seaborne use with a strengthened undercarriage, arrester hook, catapult points for deck launches and a longer nose gear leg to provide a more nose-up attitude for catapult launches. This navalized Rafale first flew in December 1991 and weighs about 500kg/1,100lb more than its land-based cousins. Catapult trials were initially carried out in July and August 1992 at NAS Lakehurst in New Jersey, USA, and Patuxent River, Maryland, USA, as France has no land-based catapult testing facility. The aircraft then undertook trials on the French carrier *Foch*.

The first flight of a production Rafale M took place in July 1999 and, on the same day, a Rafale M prototype landed on France's nuclear-powered aircraft carrier *Charles de Gaulle*. Service deliveries began in 2000 and the type officially entered

ABOVE: **With its versatile weapon-carrying capability, Rafale can combine ground-attack and air-to-air combat missions during the same sortie. It is also capable of performing multiple functions at the same time, such as Beyond Visual Range (BVR) air-to-air firing during the very-low-altitude penetration phase. This gives the Rafale impressively broad multi-role capabilities, along with a high degree of survivability.**

service in December 2000 although the first squadron, Flotille 12, did not actually reform until May 2001.The unit embarked on the *Charles de Gaulle* in 2002 and become fully operational on June 25, 2004. This followed an extended operational evaluation which included flying limited escort and tanker missions in support of Operation 'Enduring Freedom' over Afghanistan. The Rafale M is planned in three versions: the Standard F1, F2 and F3 for fighter, strike and multi-role missions respectively.

LEFT: **The M88-2 is a new-generation engine featuring state-of-the-art technologies, including a non-polluting combustion chamber. It also features the latest advances in reducing electromagnetic and infrared signatures. This very compact powerplant, offering a high thrust-to-weight ratio and exceptional controllability, especially during acceleration, is one of very few military engines with 'green' credentials.**

Dassault Rafale M

First flight: December 12, 1991
Power: Two SNECMA 8,870kg/19,555lb afterburning thrust M88-2 augmented turbofans
Armament: One 30mm cannon plus a mixed weapons load of up to 6,000kg/13,228lb including eight Matra Mica AAMs, ASMP stand-off nuclear missile and other munitions
Size: Wingspan – 10.9m/35ft 9in
  Length – 15.30m/50ft 2in
  Height – 5.34m/17ft 6in
  Wing area – 46m^2/495sq ft
Weights: Empty – 9,800kg/21,605lb
  Maximum take-off – 16,500kg/36,373lb
Performance: Maximum speed – 2,125kph/1,320mph
  Ceiling – 20,000m/65,620ft
  Range – 1,850km/1,150 miles with maximum weapon load
  Climb – 18,290m/60,000ft per minute

de Havilland Sea Venom

Proposed by de Havilland as a successor to its Vampire, the RAF's second jet fighter, the Venom was initially designated Vampire FB.8. The design had to be substantially changed to fit the new and more powerful Ghost engine – accordingly the aircraft was given its own identity – the Venom. The first production version, the FB.1, was delivered to the RAF in December 1951 followed by the improved ejection-seat equipped FB.4 version. The Venom ultimately equipped 19 squadrons of the Royal Air Force, with the Germany-based Venoms representing a vital element of the West's Cold War defences at the time.

The naval carrier-borne version, the Sea Venom, evolved from the RAF's Venom NF2 night-fighter. The naval version featured standard 'navalizing' changes, including a tail hook, strengthened and lengthened undercarriage for deck landings, and folding wings to make it suitable for carrier stowage. The first of three Sea Venom prototypes made its first flight in 1951 and began carrier trials on board HMS *Illustrious* in July that year.

The first production version was the Sea Venom FAW. Mk 20 (Fighter All-Weather), which first flew in 1953 and of which 50 were built. Powered by a single de Havilland Ghost 103 turbojet engine, its armament was the same as the RAF version.

The next version was the FAW. Mk 21 which featured changes mirroring the RAF's NF.2A and NF.3 versions including an improved Ghost 104 engine, power-operated ailerons, improved radar, a frameless canopy for better pilot visibility and Martin Baker Mk 4 ejector seats. The most apparent visual difference between the Mk 20 and Mk 21 was the loss of the tailplane extension outboard of the tail fins in the later version. In 1958, seven FAW.21s were modified for electronic countermeasures (ECM) purposes with ECM equipment replacing the cannon.

TOP: **The Sea Venom saw a great deal of action during its time in Royal Navy service and proved itself to be a good combat aircraft. The photo shows an FAW. Mk 22.** LEFT: **A Royal Navy Sea Venom leaves a British carrier deck crowded with other Sea Venoms during the 1956 Suez campaign. Note the catapult strop falling away beneath the aircraft. Sea Venoms of Nos.809, 892 and 893 Naval Air Squadrons based on the carriers HMS *Albion* and HMS *Eagle* saw action during Suez.** ABOVE: **Following trials, later versions of the Sea Venom were equipped to carry the Firestreak, also developed by a de Havilland company. Firestreak was Britain's first effective air-to-air missile and was a passive infrared homing weapon. The aircraft is pictured on board HMS *Victorious* in 1959.**

LEFT: **WM569 was a Sea Venom FAW. Mk 21. This version featured refinements similar to those of the land-based Venom NF.2A and NF.3.** ABOVE: **The first prototype Sea Venom, WK376, did its first carrier take-off on July 9, 1951, from the deck of HMS *Illustrious*. Folding wings did not feature on test aircraft until the third prototype, WK385. Production aircraft differed to the prototypes by having, among other features, permanent wingtip fuel tanks and a windscreen wiper.**

The Sea Venom FAW. Mk 22 was the final version, powered by the 2,400kg/5,300lb thrust Ghost 105 that gave a maximum speed of 927kph/576mph at sea level and a 1135km/705-mile range. Armament consisted of four fixed 20mm guns and bombs or eight rocket-projectiles below the wings. Thirty-nine were built from 1957 to 1958 and some were later equipped with the de Havilland Firestreak air-to-air missile.

In all, 256 Sea Venoms were built for the Royal Navy. From 1959, the type began to be replaced in Royal Navy service by the Sea Vixen, an aircraft that also had the distinctive de Havilland twin-boom tail. The Sea Venom had given the Royal Navy an essential interim radar-equipped all-weather fighter force between the piston-engined Sea Hornet and the appearance of the advanced Sea Vixen.

Royal Navy Sea Venoms, in concert with RAF Venom fighter-bombers, saw action during the Suez crisis in 1956. The aircraft were from Fleet Air Arm 809, 892 and 893 Naval Air Squadrons based on the light fleet carrier HMS *Albion* and fleet carrier HMS *Eagle.* The Sea Venoms saw much action and bombed numerous targets in Egypt. RN Sea Venoms later carried out attacks against Cypriot terrorists and also saw service during the troubles in the Middle East.

From 1956, 39 Sea Venoms were supplied to the Royal Australian Navy (RAN), where they replaced the Hawker Sea Fury in service. The Sea Venom was in turn replaced in RAN service from 1967 by the A-4 Skyhawk. Meanwhile, the French company Sud-Est licence-built 121 Sea Venom FAW. Mk 20s, designated *Aquilon*, for the French Navy, who operated them until 1963.

ABOVE: **The Sea Venom in the foreground shows a number of the type's features – the large hinged cockpit canopy over side-by-side seats, the folding wings and the twin boom tail.**

de Havilland Sea Venom FAW. Mk 22

First flight: April 19, 1951 (prototype)

Power: de Havilland 2,404kg/5,300lb thrust Ghost 105 turbojet

Armament: Four 20mm cannon and provision for two Firestreak air-to-air missiles or 907kg/2,000lb of bombs or eight 27kg/60lb rocket projectiles

Size: Wingspan – 13.08m/42ft 11in
Length – 11.15m/36ft 7in
Height – 2.6m/8ft 6.25in
Wing area – 25.99m²/280sq ft

Weights: Empty – 3,992kg/8,800lb
Maximum take-off – 7,167kg/15,800lb

Performance: Maximum speed – 925kph/575mph
Ceiling – 12,190m/40,000ft
Range – 1,135km/705 miles
Climb – 1,753m/5,750ft per minute

de Havilland Sea Vixen

The Sea Venom's successor in Royal Navy service was the impressive de Havilland Sea Vixen which, when it first appeared in the early 1950s, was a match for any land-based fighter of the time. It gave the Royal Navy its first swept-wing two-seat all-weather fighter and was developed from the 1946-vintage D.H. 110 that was designed to meet the Royal Air Force specification for a land-based all-weather fighter and a Royal Navy requirement for an advanced carrier-borne all-weather fighter aircraft. Naval interest waned and the RAF requirement was ultimately filled by the Gloster Javelin.

Although it followed the Vampire/Venom-type twin-boom configuration, the Sea Vixen was a totally modern aircraft, but development delays following the high profile and tragic 1952 crash of the prototype at a Farnborough air show kept the Sea Vixen from entering Royal Navy Fleet Air Arm service until 1958.

Royal Navy interest in the D.H. 100 was rekindled in 1952 and carrier trials took place in late 1954 – the Royal Navy placed its first Sea Vixen order in January the following year. A partially navalized version first flew in June, 1955 while production of the Sea Vixen FAW. Mk 1 got underway at de Havilland's Christchurch factory – the company's Chester factory was also later involved in Sea Vixen production.

TOP: **At the time of writing this is the only airworthy Sea Vixen, a former No.899 NAS aircraft.** ABOVE: **The Sea Vixen pilot's cockpit and canopy was offset to the port side to make room for the radar operator below.** BELOW: **Showing the aircraft's wing shape to great effect, a Sea Vixen buzzes the island of the British carrier HMS *Hermes*, 1961. The Sea Vixen was the last de Havilland twin-boom type.**

The Mk 1 had a hinged radome which reduced the overall length of the aircraft for carrier stowage, power-folding wings (earlier carrier aircraft had wings folded by hand) and a hydraulically steerable nosewheel – the first production version flew on March 20, 1957. Service trials followed on board HMS *Victorious* and HMS *Centaur* during November 1958 and the type finally became operational the following year. No.892 Squadron FAA was the first Sea Vixen service unit and embarked upon the famous British carrier HMS *Ark Royal* in March 1960. The Sea Vixen was the heaviest aircraft to have entered Royal Navy service.

The aircraft was the mainstay of Royal Navy carrier-borne fighter squadrons for a decade and was the first British interceptor to dispense with guns as it was armed only with air-to-air missiles and rockets – 28 2in rockets were stored in two innovative retractable fuselage containers. For strike missions the

LEFT: **Not all carrier landings went smoothly. Here, a Sea Vixen makes contact with the crash barrier on a British carrier having failed to stop. Note the Whirlwind helicopter standing by in case the aircraft ended up in the sea and a rescue was needed.**
BELOW: **The Sea Vixen was the first British aircraft to be armed exclusively with rockets and air-to-air missiles.**

missiles could be replaced by up to 900kg/2,000lb of bombs. Sea Vixens could also carry a refuelling pack to enable them to fuel other Sea Vixens, using the 'buddy' system.

The type's remarkable nose arrangement had the pilot's cockpit offset to the port side to provide sufficient working space for a radar operator whose station was below and behind on the starboard side.

The FAW. Mk 2 was an improved version that entered service in December 1963 with No.899 Squadron. Converted Mk 1s were flown in the summer of 1962 to prove the new version and subsequently a number of Mk 1s on the production line were completed as the more advanced Mk 2. A total of 67 Mk 1s were converted to Mk 2 standard, while 29 examples were built from new. More fuel was carried in the forward sections of the tail-booms which were extended forward of the wings, and armament for this model was four Red Top AAMs in place of the Firestreaks carried by the FAW. Mk 1.

Despite the Sea Vixen's late entry into service, the aircraft gave the Royal Navy a formidable all-weather interception and surface attack capability and the type was finally retired from front-line service in 1972.

For two decades after its 'retirement', the type could still be seen flying from some UK military training establishments as Sea Vixen D. Mk 3 drones used to train radar operators by providing high-speed radar targets. 'Flown' by a pilot on the ground, these brightly coloured Sea Vixens with remote control equipment in the observer's position were the last chance to see the ultimate de Havilland twin-boomer in the air, until a privately owned example joined the British civil register and air show circuit in the early 2000s.

ABOVE: **The retirement of the Sea Vixen from the Fleet Air Arm was the end of an era for de Havilland twin-boom types in front-line British military service.**

de Havilland Sea Vixen FAW. Mk 2

First flight: September 26, 1951 (D.H.110)
Power: Two Rolls-Royce 5,094kg/11,230lb thrust Avon 208 turbojets
Armament: Four Red Top infrared homing air-to-air missiles, plus two retractable nose pods with 28 2in rocket projectiles
Size: Wingspan – 15.54m/51ft
Length – 16.94/55ft 7in
Height – 3.28m/10ft 9in
Wing area – 60.2m²/648sq ft
Weights: Empty – 9,979kg/22,000lb
Maximum take-off – 16,780kg/37,000lb
Performance: Maximum speed – 1,110kph/690mph
Ceiling – 14,630m/48,000ft
Range – 1,287km/800 miles
Climb – 12,190m/40,000ft in 8 minutes, 30 seconds

Douglas Skyraider

The Skyraider can be rightly considered to be one of the greatest combat aircraft ever and one of the most durable to have operated from a carrier deck. A World War II design as a replacement for Douglas' own Dauntless dive-bomber, this rugged aircraft fought in both Korea and in Vietnam. The prototype XBT2D-1 first flew in March 1945, and in February 1946 became the AD-1 Skyraider, the biggest single-seat aircraft in production. Designed around Wright's R-3350 engine, the Skyraider was created with the benefit of considerable combat experience. The designers' aim was to produce a very versatile aircraft which could absorb considerable battle damage and carry the widest range of available weaponry. Built like a big fighter, the Skyraider carried all its weaponry beneath its folding wings.

After carrier trials in early 1946 the Skyraider formally entered US Navy front-line service with VA-19A in December 1946.

Production of consistently improved versions continued and only 4 years into manufacturing, an incredible 22 variants had appeared. Production continued for 12 years and when it ceased in 1957, a total of 3,180 Skyraiders had been delivered to the United States Navy.

Korea is often thought of as a jet war, but the Skyraider's 10-hour loiter capability and great weapon-carrying capacity considerably outclassed any jet that was in service with UN forces at the time. The US Navy were hugely impressed by the performance of the Skyraider.

Among the versions soon appearing were the AD-2 with increased fuel and more powerful engine, and the AD-3

ABOVE: **The combat record of the Skyraider was remarkable. The type saw massive amounts of action both in Korea and during the Vietnam War.** LEFT: **France acquired a number of ex-US Navy Skyraiders, initially to replace the P-47 Thunderbolts they wanted to retire. During operations in Chad, some French aircraft dropped large quantities of empty beer bottles on rebels below. This was considered to be an innovative means of avoiding breaking the ban on non-lethal weapons imposed during the conflict.**

with a revised canopy, improved propeller and landing gear. The AD-4 had the more powerful 2,700hp R-3350 engine and greatly increased load-carrying capacity, the AD-4W was a three-seat Airborne Early Warning variant (used by the Royal Navy's Fleet Air Arm) while the AD-5 was a four-seat multi-role version. The Skyraider was strengthened to carry more and more equipment and ordnance and the AD-5 could operate at all-up weights of 11,340kg/25,000lb. The AD-5 could also be adapted for casualty evacuation or for transporting 12 troops. The AD-6 was a much-improved single-seat attack version while the AD-7 had a 3,050hp engine and even more reinforcement to the wing and undercarriage.

AD-4Ns saw considerable action with the French Armée de l'Air in Algeria and these machines were retired from French service in 1965. By then the United States was embroiled in Vietnam and following trials the Skyraider was found to be the ideal close support aircraft needed for tackling difficult ground targets. Again, the hard-hitting aircraft's loiter capability made it an obvious choice for this type of warfare. The United States Air Force, Navy and Marine Corps all operated Skyraiders in Vietnam, as did the US-trained South Vietnam Air Force. The aircraft also served as Forward Air Control (FAC) platforms, helicopter escort and rescue support missions. Never considered a dogfighter, the Skyraider had four 20mm cannon in the wings and US Navy Skyraider pilots are known to have shot down at least two MiG-17 jets over Vietnam.

In 1962, new tri-service aircraft designations were introduced so all the designations of Skyraiders then in service were changed. The AD-5 was the A-1E, the AD-5N the A-1G while the AD-6 and AD-7 became the A-1H and A-1J respectively.

As well as Britain and France, Skyraiders were also supplied to Chad who was using them in combat up to the late 1970s. The aircraft that had entered service when piston-engined warplanes were thought by some to be obsolete was still fighting more than a quarter of a century after it first entered service.

TOP: **The A-1E/AD-5 was a redesigned multi-role version of the Skyraider that had a side-by-side cockpit.** ABOVE: **Although the Skyraider looked like it belonged on a World War II carrier deck, its ruggedness and versatility kept it in use as a front-line aircraft well into the 1970s.**

ABOVE: **An AD-6/A-1H of US Navy Attack Squadron 176. The unit operated the Skyraider from 1955 to 1967, and in 1966 two aircraft from the unit fought and defeated enemy MiGs in air combat.**

Douglas A-1H (AD-6) Skyraider

First flight: March 19, 1945 (XBT2D-1)

Power: One Wright 2,700hp R-3350-26WA radial piston engine

Armament: Four wing-mounted 20mm cannon, up to 3,629kg/8,000lb of ordnance carried under wings and on one fuselage hardpoint

Size: Wingspan – 15.25m/50ft 0.25in
Length – 11.84m/38ft 10in
Height – 4.78m/15ft 8.25in
Wing area – 37.19m²/400sq ft

Weights: Empty – 5,429kg/11,968lb
Maximum take-off – 11,340kg/25,000lb

Performance: Maximum speed – 518kph/322mph
Ceiling – 8,685m/28,500ft plus
Range – 2,116km/1,315 miles
Climb – 870m/2,850ft per minute

LEFT: **The Skyray possessed record-breaking speed and climb. Note the small amount of wing folding required for carrier operations.** ABOVE: **Designed with the benefit of research undertaken by Germany during the war, the aircraft entered US Navy service over a decade after the defeat of Nazi Germany. Even today the Skyray has a futuristic look about it.** BELOW: **Described by one of its test pilots as a fighter pilot's dream, the aircraft's fundamental instability made it incredibly agile.**

Douglas F4D Skyray

Douglas had examined aerodynamic data captured from the Germans at the end of World War II. The data included extensive wind tunnel test findings concerning tailless aircraft designed by Dr Alexander Lippisch, who had developed the tailless Messerschmitt Me 163 rocket fighter. Douglas talked to Lippisch, who had also explored delta wing designs, as the company was interested in the aerodynamic efficiency that the delta configuration offered to compensate for the low power available from jet engines of the time.

In January 1947, a US Navy request for a short-range carrier-based interceptor prompted Douglas to re-evaluate the tailless concept. Their design evolved from a delta flying wing with a tailfin but no pronounced fuselage to a heart-shaped delta with a fuselage. The Navy warmed to the Douglas proposal, and the prototype XF4D-1 made its first flight on January 21, 1951, from Muroc (later Edwards) Air Force Base, with Larry Peyton as test pilot. The aircraft's similarity to the ray fish led to its name.

The F4D-1's capabilities were evident when, on October 3, 1953, the second prototype set a new world air-speed record of 1211.7kph/752.9mph. Deliveries to the US Navy began in April 1956 and 17 front-line US Navy/USMC units, plus three reserve units, were eventually equipped with the Skyray.

The Skyray's deep delta wing roots contained the air intakes feeding the single turbojet, fuel for which was contained both in the wings and the fuselage. Leading-edge slats were fitted for increased lift during take-off and landing.

Known to its crews as the 'Ford' (after the 'four' and 'D' of its designation), this aircraft had a spectacular rate and angle of climb and set five new time-to-altitude records. It saw the

Skyray fly from a complete stop to 15,240m/50,000ft in 2 minutes and 36.05 seconds. This performance led to one Skyray-equipped US Navy unit, VFAW-3 based at Naval Air Station North Island in California, being part of North American Air Defense Command tasked with defending the US from Soviet bombers – the only US Navy unit to do so.

Engine development problems meant that production aircraft were not delivered to the US Navy until early 1956 while the US Marine Corps received their first in 1957. This was an unusually long development period for a time when aerospace innovation was progressing at breakneck speed rendering designs obsolete very quickly.

The production Skyray was fitted with the Aero-13 fire-control system which featured the Westinghouse AN/APQ-50 radar. Impressive for its time, this radar had a normal detection range of 29km/18 miles, and a lock-on range of 20km/12 miles. Pilots admired the Skyray's capabilities. It was very manoeuvrable and possessed an impressive rate of roll but it was a handful for a relatively inexperienced pilot. Keeping the unstable aircraft level was a constant challenge – these days, digital fly-by-wire flight control systems would easily tame the Skyray.

VFAW-3 Skyrays deployed to Florida during the Cuban Missile Crisis in 1962, protecting US air space from Cuban intruders. Radar contact was made with MiGs but no confrontations resulted.

Designed exclusively for the high-altitude interception role, the Skyray was unsuited to the multi-mission capabilities required by the mid-1960s so it had a fairly short service life. The last aircraft were withdrawn from service from 1964, but a single example was used by NASA until 1969, and the US Navy Test Pilots School at Patuxent River in Maryland kept one airworthy to give students experience of how an unstable aircraft flew. In 1962, some Skyrays were fitted out as target drone controllers and redesignated DF-6A.

A total of 420 were built by the time production ended in December 1958. The type was redesignated F-6A when the United States military rationalized aircraft designations in September 1962. A Skyray development, the F5D Skylancer, was designed and prototypes were built, but it was cancelled before production began.

ABOVE: **The aircraft was certainly a handful, and never required more attention than during carrier landings. The mainwheel legs lowered separately, and as the first leg generated drag, the aircraft would start to 'skid' in the air.**

BELOW: **The high angle of attack required on landing meant that the large wing area 'blanked' out the tail from the airflow, which reduced the fin's effect on the aircraft's control. The aircraft was best suited to pilots who liked a challenge every time they flew the type. Today's fly-by-wire technology would have made the Skyray much easier to fly.**

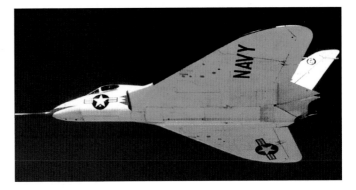

ABOVE: **The Skyray had the Aero-13 fire-control system which featured a Westinghouse AN/APQ-50 radar. Advanced for its time, the radar had a detection range of around 29km/18 miles.**

Douglas F4D Skyray

First flight: January 23, 1951
Power: Pratt & Whitney 6,577kg/14,500lb afterburning thrust J57-P-8B turbojet
Armament: Four 20mm/0.78in cannon, plus up to 1,814kg/4,000lb of fuel or ordnance on six underwing hardpoints
Size: Wingspan – 10.21m/33ft 6in
Length – 13.93m/45ft 8.25in
Height – 3.96m/13ft
Wing area – 51.75m²/557sq ft
Weights: Empty – 7,268kg/16,024lb
Maximum take-off – 11,340kg/25,000lb
Performance: Maximum speed – 1,162kph/722mph
Ceiling – 16,765m/55,000ft
Range – 1,931km/1,200 miles
Climb – 5,580m/18,300ft

Douglas A-3 Skywarrior

By the late 1940s, a whole new class of aircraft carrier was under development by the US Navy, the Forrestal supercarrier class. These enormous carriers would be able to operate large aircraft and give the US Navy the opportunity to take airpower to a new level. The Navy called for a large new strategic bomber to operate from the supercarriers and Douglas came up with the A3D, at 31,750kg/70,000lb the world's largest and heaviest carrier-borne aircraft when it was designed. The nuclear bomb aspect was challenging for the aircraft design team because details of the weapon were top secret, and designers had to guess the appearance and weight of the nuclear bombs to be carried on board. In its vast internal bomb bay, it could carry up to 5,400kg/12,000lb of weaponry. Also, the internal bomb bay had to be accessible from the cockpit, so the crew could arm the nuclear device during flight. The type first flew in October 1952, and went on to become the US Navy's first twin-jet nuclear bomber.

The first production version, the A3D-1 (later redesignated A-3A), with a radar-controlled tail turret and a crew of three, first joined US Navy fleet squadrons on March 31, 1956 when

ABOVE: **The Skywarrior was among the longest serving US Navy strike aircraft; having entered service in the mid-1950s and not being retired until 1991.**
BELOW: **Before the US Navy's Polaris submarines entered service, the Skywarrior was a vital element of the service's nuclear capability.**

five A3D-1s were delivered to Heavy Attack Squadron One (VAH-1) at NAS Jacksonville, Florida. In April 1956, VAH-2 became the Pacific Fleet's first Skywarrior unit.

The first deployment of the A3D-1 was during the Suez Crisis – on November 7, 1956, VAH-1's A3Ds were taken aboard USS *Forrestal* which then sailed for the Eastern Atlantic. The first major depoyment was in January 1957 when VAH-1 took the Skywarrior aboard the USS *Forrestal* on a cruise to the Mediterranean. These aircraft were not, however, combat-ready and were still establishing the parameters for the operation of these large jet-powered aircraft aboard aircraft carriers.

The A3D-2 began to reach fleet squadrons in 1957 and was used to set some impressive records – on March 21, 1957, an A3D-2 travelling west set a US transcontinental speed record with a time of 5 hours, 12 minutes, and a

ABOVE: **For storage below deck, the A-3's wings could fold almost flat, hinged outboard of the engines. Even the tall tail was hinged and would fold to starboard.** RIGHT: **This aircraft is one of 30 A3D-2P reconnaissance variants produced. The weapons bay carried up to 12 cameras plus photoflash bombs and had a crew of three – pilot, co-pilot/photo-navigator and photo technician/gunner/ECM operator. Note the camera fairings on the side of the forward fuselage.**

Los Angeles–New York–Los Angeles speed record of 9 hours, 31 minutes. On June 6, a pair of Skywarriors took off from a carrier off the coast of California, flew across the US and landed four hours later on another carrier stationed off the east coast of Florida. The A3D-1 and the A3D-2 ultimately equipped 13 US Navy VAH squadrons, including two training units.

By the late 1950s, Skywarrior versions included the specialized and primarily land-based electronic reconnaissance A3D-2Q (later known as the EA-3B), the photographic reconnaissance A3D-2P (redesignated RA-3B), and the A3D-2T trainer (TA-3B). The last of 283 Skywarriors left the production line in January 1961 and in 1962 the aircraft was redesignated A-3 by which time, due to its size, it had been christened 'Whale' by its crews.

By 1965 the Skywarrior was in action over Vietnam, initially as a conventional bomber dropping 'iron' bombs, although mining missions were flown later. It was, however, as tanker aircraft that most Skywarriors saw service in South-east Asia.

Eighty-five A-3Bs had their bombing kit removed and permanently replaced by tanker equipment – these aircraft were redesignated KA-3Bs. Later, a number of these were modified for combined electronic countermeasures/aerial tanker use and were redesignated EKA-3B. Tanker Skywarriors, who helped aircraft short of fuel or damaged return to their base or carrier, were credited with saving over 700 aircraft from loss during the course of the Vietnam war.

As advancing technology rendered its old bombing role obsolete, the resilient aircraft's evolution kept it in service for many years. The EA-3B was withdrawn from US carrier use in December 1987 but a few Skywarriors served in the 1991 Gulf War.

A substantially revised US Air Force version of the Skywarrior was named the Destroyer and designated B-66. Douglas built 294 B-66 Destroyers in bomber, photo-recon, electronic countermeasures and weather reconnaissance versions, many of which were active in the Vietnam War.

ABOVE: **The largest and heaviest carrier-borne aircraft of its day – the A-3 Skywarrior. Note the lack of the defensive tail gun, which was deleted in later versions of the A-3.**

Douglas A-3B Skywarrior

First flight: October 28, 1952 (XA3D-1)

Power: Two Pratt & Whitney 4,763kg/10,500lb thrust J57-P-10 turbojets

Armament: Two 20mm cannon in remotely controlled rear turret plus up to 5,443kg/12,000lb of bombs

Size: Wingspan – 22.1m/72ft 6in
Length – 23.27m/76ft 4in
Height – 6.95m/22ft 9.5in
Wing area – 75.43m²/812sq ft

Weights: Empty – 17,876kg/39,409lb
Maximum take-off – 37,195kg/82,000lb

Performance: Maximum speed – 982kph/610mph
Ceiling – 12,495m/41,000ft
Range – 1,690km/1,050 miles
Climb – 1,100m/3,600ft per minute

LEFT: **The unusual and distinctive Fairey Gannet was a vital aircraft in the Royal Navy's Cold War inventory, and provided anti-submarine and then Airborne Early Warning protection across a 23-year period. Note the 'finlets'.**

Fairey Gannet

From hard lessons during World War II, the Royal Navy had learned the value of carrier-based anti-submarine aircraft. For the post-war years the Navy needed a modern aircraft to tackle the submarine threat posed to Britain's navy and its interests by any potential enemy. In 1945 the Fleet Air Arm issued a requirement, GR.17/45, for a carrier-based Anti-Submarine Warfare (ASW) aircraft that could both hunt and kill submarines.

Of two cosmetically similar designs (the other from Blackburn) built to prototype standard, it was the Fairey 17 that ultimately won the contract having flown for the first time on September 19, 1949. The aircraft had a deep barrel-like fuselage to accommodate both sensors and weapons for hunting and killing enemy craft. Power came from an Armstrong Siddeley Double Mamba engine which was actually two turboprop engines driving a shared gearbox, which in turn drove a contra-rotating propeller system. The Double Mamba was chosen as one of the engines could be shut down for more economical cruising flight. Conventional twin-engined aircraft exhibit problematic handling if one engine fails, resulting in what is known as 'asymmetric flight' when the working engine forces its side of the aeroplane ahead of the other side resulting in a crabbing flightpath as well as major concerns on landing. If 'half' of a Double Mamba failed this would not be an issue for the pilot of the 'single-engined' Gannet.

The Fairey 17 began carrier deck trials in early 1950, and on June 19 that year the aircraft made the first landing of a turboprop aircraft on a carrier – HMS *Illustrious*. The Admiralty then requested that search radar be included as well as a third seat for its operator which resulted in a third modified prototype that flew in May 1951. When Fairey's aircraft won the competition to go into production, the name Gannet was given to the aircraft. The Gannet, brimming with equipment and weapons, was a technically complicated aircraft, an example being the wings that folded not once but twice for below-deck stowage. Due to development delays, the Gannet AS.1 did not enter Fleet Air Arm service until 1955, some ten years after the requirement was first issued.

The Gannet's fuselage had a big weapons bay to accommodate two torpedoes or other munitions, up to a maximum weapon load of 900kg/2,000lb. A retractable radome under the rear fuselage housed the search radar. When the extendable 'dustbin' radome was added, it led to lateral instability in flight, which was remedied by the addition of two auxiliary finlets to the horizontal tailplane. Simply raising the height of the vertical tailplane would have had the same effect but would have exceeded below-deck hangar height limits. The Gannet's crew of three sat in

ABOVE: **The Fairey Gannet was a large and tall aircraft and required a complex wing-folding mechanism to enable the aircraft to fit below the decks of Royal Navy aircraft carriers.**

LEFT: **XL494 was an Airborne Early Warning variant, the Gannet AEW.3, a completely new design with a different tail. The bulbous radome under the fuselage housed the AN/APS20 radar.**

BELOW: **An excellent air-to-air study of a Gannet AS.1. Note the three cockpit canopies, the gull-wing and the engine's jetpipe forward of the roundel.**

tandem, with pilot, observer/navigator, and radio/radar operator each in their own cockpits, the radio-radar operator's seat facing the tail of the aircraft.

A number of Gannets were operated by foreign air arms. Deliveries to the Royal Australian Navy for carrier operations began in 1955 (phased out in 1967), while the former West German naval air arm operated Gannets from shore bases, phasing them out in 1965. Indonesia obtained refurbished Royal Navy examples.

A total of 181 Gannet AS.1s were built together with 38 Gannet T.2 conversion trainers for training pilots on the idiosyncrasies of the aircraft and its unique powerplant. In 1956, the improved 3,035hp Double Mamba 101 was introduced into Gannets on the production line. Aircraft powered by the 101 were designated AS.4 and T.5 for the trainer version. The Gannet AS.6 was the AS.4 with a new 1961 radar and electronics fit to keep it effective.

Fairey were also contracted to produce an Airborne Early Warning (AEW) Gannet to replace the Douglas Skyraider in

Fleet Air Arm service. Designated AEW.3, these were new-build dedicated early warning aircraft mounting a huge radar installation on the underside of the fuselage beneath the cockpit. This version, which served until 1978, carried a pilot and two radar plotters who were housed in a rear cabin.

ABOVE: **The Gannet AS.1 had a large weapons bay, big enough to accommodate two torpedoes. The version had a retractable 'dustbin' ventral radome that housed a search radar.**

Fairey Gannet AS.1

First flight: September 19, 1949 (prototype)
Power: One Armstrong Siddeley 2,950eshp Double Mamba 100 turboprop
Armament: Up to 907kg/2,000lb of torpedoes, depth charges
Size: Wingspan – 16.56m/54ft 4in
  Length – 13.11m/43ft
  Height – 4.18m/13ft 8.5in
  Wing area – 44.85m²/483sq ft
Weights: Empty – 6,835kg/15,069lb
  Maximum take-off – 9,798kg/21,600lb
Performance: Maximum speed – 499kph/310mph
  Ceiling – 7,620m/25,000ft
  Range – 1,518km/943 miles
  Climb – 670m/2,200ft per minute

Grumman A-6 Intruder

Designed for a 1957 US Navy competition, the Grumman A-6 Intruder was a two-seat all-weather, subsonic, carrier-based attack aircraft. While the performance of the subsonic A-6 was not spectacular, it was superbly suited to the particular attack role for which it was carefully tailored. The prototype made its first test flight in April 1960 and was followed by 482 production A-6As delivered to the US Navy from early 1963.

TOP: **A US Navy A-6 about to be bombed-up with mines on the deck of a US carrier. The Intruder was capable of carrying a staggering array of weaponry, which made it extremely useful to military planners. Note the folded wings and the integral fold-down ladder beneath the cockpit.** ABOVE: **The Prowler was developed specifically for use over Vietnam.**

From night flights over the jungles of Vietnam to Desert Storm missions above heavily fortified targets in Iraq, the Grumman A-6 Intruder developed a work-horse reputation and was the subject of many tales of daring aviation during its 34-year career as the US Navy's principal medium-attack aircraft. The aircraft's ruggedness and all-weather mission capability made it a formidable asset to US Navy and Marine Corps air wings throughout its service. The strengths of the Intruder included its ability to fly in any weather and its heavy weapons payload – two traits highlighted on the big screen in the 1991 action film *Flight of the Intruder*. A little-known fact is that the Intruder delivered more ordnance during the Vietnam War than the B-52.

A tough and versatile aircraft, the A-6 was called upon to fly the most difficult missions, with flying low and alone in any weather its specialty. The all-weather attack jet saw action in every conflict the US has been involved in since Vietnam. With the ability to carry more ordnance, launch a wider variety of smart weapons, conduct day or night strikes over greater distances on internal fuel than any carrier-borne aircraft before

or since, and provide mid-air refuelling support to other carrier jets, the Intruder is considered by some to be the most versatile military aircraft of modern times.

In 1986 the A-6E, an advanced upgraded development of the A-6A, proved that it was the best all-weather precision bomber in the world in the joint strike on Libyan terrorist-related targets. With US Air Force F-111s, A-6E Intruders penetrated sophisticated Libyan air-defence systems, which had been alerted by the high level of diplomatic tension and by rumours of impending attacks. Evading over 100 guided missiles, the strike force flew at a low level in complete darkness, and accurately delivered laser-guided and other ordnance on target.

No guns of any kind were carried aboard the A-6, and the aircraft had no internal bomb bay. A wide variety of stores,

LEFT: **Two A-6 Intruders operating from the USS *Constellation* during the Vietnam War. Note the sheer number of bombs (18 Mk 82 free fall) each aircraft is carrying and the blackened airbrakes under the word 'Navy'.** ABOVE: **The Intruder was finally retired in 1997.**

however, could be mounted externally, including both conventional and nuclear bombs, fuel tanks, and an assortment of rockets and missiles. As with all versatile attack aircraft, many combinations of payload and mission radius were available to the A-6E. For example, a weapons load of 945kg/2,080lb consisting of a Mk 43 nuclear bomb could be delivered at a mission radius of 1,432km/890 miles. For that mission, four 1,136-litre/300-US gallon external tanks are carried. Alternatively, a bomb load of 4,676kg/10,296lb could be delivered at a mission radius of 724km/450 miles with two 1,136-litre/300-US gallon external tanks. Intruders were retired from front-line service in the late 1990s.

The EA-6B Prowlers were developed from the EA-6A which was an Intruder airframe intended primariliy to be an electronic countermeasures and intelligence-gathering platform. These aircraft were initially designed to fly in support of the Intruders on Vietnam missions. The EA-6B is, however, a significant aircraft in its own right and provides an umbrella of protection for strike aircraft (by suppressing enemy air defences), ground troops and ships by jamming enemy radar, electronic data links and communications. At the same time, the Prowler is gathering tactical electronic intelligence within the combat area. The EA-6B has proven itself in Vietnam, the Middle East, South-west Asia and the Balkans, where strike aircraft losses were dramatically reduced when the Prowler was on station.

As a result of 'restructuring of US military assets' in 1995, the EF-111 Raven was retired and the EA-6B was left as the sole tactical radar support jammer in the US inventory. At the time of writing, eight expeditionary squadrons are now available to the US Commanders in Chief – four Navy squadrons with US Air Force aircrews and four US Marine Corps. The United States Department of Defense describes the Prowler as 'a unique national asset' – the type will fly on for the foreseeable future.

ABOVE: **This A-6 Intruder shows the later wing-tip mounted airbrakes deployed. The United States Navy and Marine Corps were the only operators of the type.**

Grumman A-6E Intruder

First flight: April 19, 1960 (YA-6A)

Power: Two Pratt & Whitney 4,218kg/9,300lb thrust J52-P-8B turbojets

Armament: Up to 8,165kg/18,000lb of nuclear or conventional ordnance or missiles

Size: Wingspan – 16.15m/53ft
Length – 16.69m/54ft 9in
Height – 4.93m/16ft 2in
Wing area – 49.13m²/529sq ft

Weights: Empty – 12,093kg/26,660lb
Maximum catapult take-off – 2,6581kg/58,600lb

Performance: Maximum speed – 1,035kph/644mph
Ceiling – 12,925m/42,400ft
Range – 1,627km/1,011 miles
Climb – 2,621m/8,600ft per minute

Grumman F9F-2 Panther

The Panther was the US Navy's most widely used jet fighter of the Korean War and the first of the Grumman 'cats' to be jet powered. The Panther was also the first carrier-borne jet to see action. Although it was mainly used in the ground-attack role, it did notch up some air combat successes against North Korean MiGs. On July 3, 1950, a Panther of US Navy unit VF-51 aboard USS *Valley Forge* scored the US Navy's first aerial kill of the Korean war when it downed a Yak-9. By the end of the war the F9F had flown 78,000 combat missions.

Grumman's first jet fighter for the US Navy had its origins in the last days of World War II, when the US Navy Fighter Branch drew up a requirement for an all-weather/night radar-equipped carrier-borne fighter. As originally planned, Grumman's proposed XF9F-1 was powered by no less than four jet engines positioned in the wings. The high number of engines was dictated by the low power output of early

ABOVE: **The Panther was operated by the US Navy and US Marine Corps and was the mount of the famous Blue Angels. Reconditioned Panthers were sold to Argentina but were only used from land bases.** BELOW LEFT: **The wings folded hydraulically from just outboard of the main gear but the wing fold angle was well short of the vertical. Two 454-litre/120-US gallon fuel tanks were permanently mounted on the wingtips of production versions.**

turbojets. That many engines called for a wingspan of almost 17m/55.7ft which concerned Grumman – they knew that their twin-engine Tigercat had already proved large for carrier operations.

The US Navy were aware of British jet developments and imported two Rolls-Royce Nenes for testing. They were so impressed that the Grumman design was refined and when the prototype XF9F-2 Panther flew on November 24, 1947, it was powered by a lone Rolls-Royce Nene engine. In the same year, US engine giant Pratt & Whitney acquired a licence and produced their own Nene as the J42 which went on to power a number of US military aircraft. The type's distinctive 454-litre/120-US gallon wingtip fuel tanks were first tested in February 1948 and were adopted as standard to extend the aircraft's range. The straight-wing F9F-2 went into production and was equipping US naval units by mid-1949 having completed carrier trials two months earlier. The type proved popular with pilots who praised its handling, performance and reliability.

The Panther had a large fuselage to accommodate the large diameter engines of the time and two big internal fuel tanks, which enabled the aircraft to carry twice as much as fuel as the Hawker Sea Hawk still on the drawing board at the time. An

ejection seat was fitted in the pressurized cockpit while the nose contained radio equipment and four 20mm cannon. Later -2s had underwing racks for two 454kg/1,000lb bombs and six 5in rockets for service in Korea. For a time the attack version of the -2 was designated F9F-2B but as most were modified for attack missions, the B was dropped.

A small number of Panther F9F-3s were built powered by the Allison J33 but these were later converted to -2 standard by the installation of the J42 engine. A total of 109 examples of the -4 were ordered, but powerplant (Allison J33-A-16) issues led to most being completed to -5 standard.

The F9F-5 with its lengthened (by 0.61m/2ft) fuselage and taller fin were powered by the J48 (a licence-built Rolls-Royce Tay) featuring water injection and 3,175kg/7,000lb thrust. Having first flown as the XF9F-5 in December 1949, the longer fuselage could hold a further 2,888 litres/763 US gallons of fuel. This was the most produced Panther, and a number of these machines became F9F-5P reconnaissance versions.

F9F-5 Panthers continued in front-line US Navy service until October 1958, when VAH-7 retired their last machines. The type did, however, continue to equip training units into the 1960s, while the F9F-5KD/DF-9E was used for drone work in missile trials. In 1966 a batch of F9F-2s were reconditioned as fighters, and were supplied to the Argentine Navy.

TOP: **Panthers operating from the deck of the USS *Bon Homme Richard* CV-31. The carrier first deployed to the Western Pacific for actions against targets in Korea in May 1951 and remained on station until December 1951. The carrier and its Panthers returned for the same period in 1952.** ABOVE: **Rocket-armed Panthers from USS *Boxer*, CV-21, over Wonsan in 1951. This was the scene of the large-scale UN landing.** LEFT: **A F9F-2B Panther armed with six 5in High-Velocity Aircraft Rockets (HVARs). On landing approach, the arrester hook would first be extended then lowered, ready to catch the wire.** BELOW LEFT: **An F9F-2B of VF-112 'Fighting Twelve' during the unit's time in the Korean War.**

Grumman F9F-2B Panther

First flight: November 24, 1947
Power: Pratt & Whitney 2,586kg/5,700lb thrust J42-P-8 turbojet (licence-built R-R Nene)
Armament: Four 20mm cannon plus underwing weapon load of up to 907kg/2,000lb
Size: Wingspan – 11.58m/37ft 11.75in
Length – 11.35m/37ft 3in
Height – 3.45m/11ft 4in
Wing area –23.22m²/250sq ft
Weights: Empty – 4,533kg/9,993lb
Maximum take-off – 8,842kg/19,494lb
Performance: Maximum speed – 877kph/545mph
Ceiling – 13,590m/44,600ft
Range – 2,177km/1,353 miles
Climb – 1,567m/5,140ft per minute

Grumman F9F Cougar

Grumman, aware of wartime German swept-wing research, had considered a swept-wing version of the F9F in December 1945. In March 1950 the company sought official approval for a swept-wing version of the Panther – Grumman was given the green light for this logical and speedy development of an already successful programme. Having been granted a contract in March 1951, Grumman tested the first swept-wing aircraft of the F9F family (still a modified Panther) on September 20, 1951.

It was different enough from the Panther to warrant the new Cougar name but the US Navy really considered it to be just a swept-wing version of the Panther, hence the F9F designation – in fact only the forward fuselage was retained from the original straight-winged aircraft. The wings had 35 degrees sweep and the wingtip fuel tanks were deleted – power was provided by the J48-8 engine with water/alcohol injection giving a thrust of 3,289kg/7,250lb.

An initial production run of 646 F9F-6s were delivered to the US Navy between mid-1952 and July 1954. Armament consisted of four 20mm cannon in the nose while two 454kg/1,000lb bombs could be carried under the wings, as could 570-litre/150-US gallon drop tanks. The Cougar entered US Navy service in late 1952 and, unlike the straight-winged Panther, would not have been outclassed by Russian MiG-15s had it seen Korean War service. Sixty Cougars were built as F9F-6P reconnaissance versions fitted with cameras instead of the cannon in the nose.

The F9F-7 version (later redesignated F-9H in 1962), powered by the 2,880kg/6,350lb J33 engine, reached a production total of 168. The J33 proved to be disappointing and unreliable so almost all were converted to take the reliable J48 engines, thus becoming indistinguishable from the earlier F9F-6s.

The F9F-8 (later redesignated F-9J) was the final production version of the fighter. It featured a 200mm/8in-longer fuselage and bigger, modified wings with greater chord and wing area for better low-speed, high angle of attack flying and to give increased room for fuel tanks. The F9F-8 first flew in December 1953 and in January 1954 exceeded the speed of sound in a shallow dive. A total of 601 of these

ABOVE: **The F9F-6 Cougar replaced the Panther in service with the US Navy Blue Angels aerobatics team but these aircraft were withdrawn when problems developed so the team reverted back to the F9F–5 Panther until December 1954 when they acquired the newer F9F-8 model.** LEFT: **The F9F-8 was in more ways than one the ultimate version of the fighter. This version had six hardpoints for fuel tanks and missiles and is shown here armed with four Sidewinders.**

aircraft were delivered between April 1954 and March 1957 – most were equipped for inflight refuelling, and late production examples could carry four AIM-9 Sidewinder air-to-air missiles beneath the wings. Most earlier aircraft were then modified to this configuration. A number of F9F-8s were even fitted with nuclear bombing equipment. F9F-8s were withdrawn from front-line service in 1958–59 to be replaced by the F8U Crusader and F11F Tiger.

The F9F-8B (later the AF-9J) were F9F-8s converted into single-seat attack-fighters while 110 photo-reconnaissance versions, the F9F-8P, were also delivered in 1955–57. The US Navy acquired 377 two-seat F9F-8T (later TF-9J) trainers between 1956 and 1960 for use as advanced trainers and for weapons and carrier training – they served until 1974. Armed with twin 20mm cannon they could also carry bombs or missiles. This was the only version of the Cougar to see action – they were used in the airborne command role during 1966 and 1967, directing air strikes in South Vietnam. After withdrawal from active service, many Cougars were used

as unmanned drones (F9F-6K) for combat training or as drone directors (F9F-6D) – these were later redesignated QF-9F and DF-9F respectively. Two-seat trainer versions of the Cougar were still flying in US Navy service in the mid-1970s.

The only other air arm to use the Cougar was the Argentine Navy who also operated the Panther. An Argentine Cougar was the first aircraft to break the sound barrier in that country.

TOP AND ABOVE: **The F9F-8T was a two-seat carrier-capable trainer version of the F9F-8 that retained some of cannon armament of the single-seat version – the student sat in front, instructor in the rear. The F9F-8T entered service with the Naval Air Training Command (NATC) in 1957 and eventually equipped five squadrons. The F9F-8T (later the TF-9J) played an important role in training most of the pilots who were later to fly combat missions in Vietnam.**

ABOVE: **The Cougar and earlier Panther were powered mainly by engines derived from powerplants developed by Frank Whittle in the UK but it was US engineers who really maximized the output of the licence-built Nene.**

Grumman F9F-8 Cougar

First flight: September 20, 1951

Power: Pratt & Whitney 3,266kg/7,200lb thrust J48-P-8A turbojet

Armament: Two 20mm cannon plus 907kg/2,000lb of underwing weapons

Size: Wingspan – 10.52m/34ft 6in
Length – 13.54m/44ft 5in including probe
Height – 3.73m/12ft 3in
Wing area – 31.31m^2/337sq ft

Weights: Empty – 5,382kg/11,866lb
Maximum take-off – 11,232kg/24,763lb

Performance: Maximum speed – 1,041kph/647mph
Ceiling – 15,240m/50,000ft
Range – 1,610km/1,000 miles
Climb – 1,860m/6,100ft per minute

Grumman F-14 Tomcat

Despite its age, the swing-wing, twin-engine Grumman F-14 Tomcat remained one of the world's most potent interceptors until its retirement. Its primary missions, in all weathers, were air superiority, fleet air defence and, latterly, precision strikes against ground targets. Continued developments and improvements maintained its capabilities to the extent that it was still a potent threat and an effective deterrent to any hostile aircraft foolish enough to threaten US Navy aircraft carrier groups. Its mix of air-to-air weapons was unmatched by any other interceptor type, and its radar was the most capable long-range airborne interception radar carried by any fighter of the time. With its mix of weapons it could attack any target at any altitude from ranges between only a few hundred feet to over 160km/100 miles away.

The F-14 had its beginnings in the early 1960s when Grumman collaborated with General Dynamics on the abortive F-111B, the carrier-based escort fighter version of the F-111. Even before the F-111B cancellation took place, Grumman began work on a company-funded project known as Design 303, a carrier-borne aircraft for the air superiority, escort fighter, and deck-launched interception role.

Having flown for the first time on December 21, 1970, the first two US Navy F-14 squadrons were formed in 1972 and

ABOVE: **Wings swept back for high-speed flight, the F-14 was at the top of its game for over three decades and posed a major threat to any aircraft foolish enough to engage it.** BELOW LEFT: **On the deck of the USS *Saratoga*, a Tomcat is readied for flight. A Phoenix AAM with a protective shroud over its radome awaits loading on a weapons trolley.**

went to sea in 1974, making the Tomcat the first variable-geometry carrier-borne aircraft in service. Its variable-geometry wings were designed for both speed and greater stability. In full forward-sweep position, the wings provided the lift needed for slow-speed flight, especially needed during carrier landings. In swept-back positions, the wings blended into the aircraft, giving the F-14 a dart-like configuration for high-speed supersonic flight.

The F-14 Tomcat was designed to carry a million-dollar missile, the AIM-54 Phoenix, and was the only aircraft armed with the AIM-54. With a range of over 200km/120 miles, the AIM-54 gave the Tomcat a very long-range punch. Enemy aircraft could be engaged before the Tomcat even appeared on its opponents' radar screens. Less expensive Sidewinders were also carried for close air fighting.

The F-14B, introduced in November 1987, incorporated new General Electric F-110 engines. A 1995 upgrade programme was initiated to incorporate new digital avionics and weapon system improvements to strengthen the F-14's multi-mission capability. The vastly improved F-14D, delivered from 1990, was a major upgrade with F-110 engines, new APG-71 radar system, Airborne Self-Protection Jammer (ASPJ), Joint Tactical Information Distribution System (JTIDS) and Infra-Red Search and Track (IRST). Additionally, all F-14 variants were given precision strike capability using the LANTIRN (Low-Altitude Navigation and Targeting Infra-Red for Night) targeting system, night-vision compatibility, new defensive countermeasures systems and a new digital flight control

LEFT: **The F-14 could carry six examples of the Phoenix and was the only aircraft that carried the 'million-dollar missile' in service.** ABOVE: **An F-14 of US Navy unit VF-103 with its wings spread for lower-speed flight. The type's starring role in the film *Top Gun* suddenly made the Tomcat known to millions the world over.**

system. LANTIRN pods, placed on an external point beneath the right wing, allowed the F-14 to drop laser-guided bombs under the cover of darkness. The improved F-14B and F-14D were built and deployed by the US Navy in modest numbers.

The Tomcat first got to prove itself in combat on August 19, 1981, when two F-14s from the USS *Nimitz* were 'intercepted' by two Libyan Sukhoi Su-22 fighter-bombers. The Libyan jets apparently attacked the F-14s and were destroyed with ease. Again on January 4, 1989, two Libyan MiG-23 'Floggers' were engaged by two F-14s and shot down.

Tomcats also saw combat during Operation 'Desert Storm' providing top cover protection for bombers and other aircraft, and performing TARPS (Tactical Air Reconnaissance Pod System) missions – the TARPS-equipped F-14 was the US Navy's only manned tactical reconnaissance platform at the time. In late 1995 the F-14 Tomcat was used in the bomber role against targets in Bosnia. Nicknamed 'Bombcats', the F-14s dropped laser-guided 'smart' bombs while other aircraft illuminated the targets with lasers.

At one time it was thought that the F-14 would remain in service to at least 2008, but the high cost of upgrades and maintenance finally led to the retirement of the type that epitomized 'Top Gun' in late 2006. The last F-14 combat mission was completed over Iraq on February 8, 2006. During their final deployment on the USS *Theodore Roosevelt*, Tomcat units VF-31 and VF-213 collectively completed 1,163 combat sorties totaling 6,876 flight hours, and dropped 4,300kg/9,500lb of ordnance during reconnaissance, surveillance, and close air support missions in support of Operation 'Iraqi Freedom'. The last flight of the F-14 Tomcat in US service took place on October 4, 2006, when an F-14D of VF-31 was ferried to Republic Airport on Long Island, New York.

A total of 79 of the type were even exported to Iran before the downfall of the Shah and a number were thought to still be in service in 2007, despite having been without the benefit of US technical back-up since 1980.

Grumman F-14 Tomcat

First flight: December 21, 1970
Power: Two Pratt & Whitney 9,480kg/20,900lb afterburning thrust TF30-P-412A turbofans
Armament: One 20mm cannon plus six AIM-7F Sparrow and four AIM-9 Sidewinder AAMs, or six AIM-54A Phoenix long-range AAMs and two AIM-9s, or a variety of air-to-surface weapons up to 6,575kg/14,500lb
Size: Wingspan – 19.55m/64ft 1.5in unswept
Length – 19.1m/62ft 8in
Height – 4.88m/16ft
Wing area – 52.49m²/565sq ft
Weights: Empty – 18,036kg/39,762lb
Maximum take-off – 31,945kg/70,426lb
Performance: Maximum speed – 2,486kph/1,545mph
Ceiling – 18,290m/60,000ft
Range – 725km/450 miles
Climb – 18,290m/60,000ft in 2 minutes, 6 seconds

ABOVE: **The range of weaponry that the F-14 could carry was formidable, and included long, medium and short-range air-to-air missiles, air-to-ground weapons and even mines.**

Grumman F11F Tiger

While the Grumman Cougar was making its first flight, Grumman designers were already hard at work on an aerodynamically advanced supersonic successor (known to Grumman as the G-98) derived from the Cougar/Panther family. It became clear that a simple redesign of the Cougar would not meet the requirements and the G-98 evolved into a completely different aircraft with no resemblance to the Cougar.

The resulting aircraft was the smallest and lightest aircraft that could be designed for the day-fighter mission. The reduced size had another advantage – only the wingtips needed to be folded for carrier handling and storage thus eliminating the need for complex heavy wing-folding gear. The Wright J65 engine, a licence-built version of the British Armstrong Siddeley Sapphire, was fed by a pair of intakes mounted on the fuselage sides behind the cockpit, which was located well forward on the

ABOVE: **Power for the Tiger came from a licensed development of the British Sapphire engine. As well as undergoing some redesign the engine was, in the case of some US Navy examples, fitted with an afterburner too.**

BELOW LEFT: **The second Tiger prototype, equipped with an afterburning engine, became the second supersonic US Navy aircraft to break the sound barrier. Despite early promise, the F11F's front-line career only lasted four years.**

nose and had a rear-sliding canopy. The sloping nose gave the pilot good forward visibility – an important factor when landing on a pitching carrier deck moving in all directions. A retractable tailskid was included to minimize damage to the rear fuselage in the event of a nose-high landing. By now designated the XF9F-9, the aircraft took to the air for the first time on July 30, 1954, with Grumman test pilot 'Corky' Meyer at the controls.

During the long and troubled development period that followed, the aircraft eventually got a new designation – the F11F – and, in keeping with Grumman's feline traditions, the name Tiger. The engine's afterburner problems continued and a de-rated engine was fitted to get the aircraft into service.

The first catapult launchings and carrier landings took place aboard the USS *Forrestal* in April, 1956. During service trials, the range and endurance of the Tiger were found to be inadequate so the second production batch featured additional fuel tanks built into the engine intake walls and fin, increasing internal fuel capacity from 3,460 litres/914 US gallons to 3,971 litres/1,049 US gallons. A 1.8m/6ft-longer nose was also fitted to later production examples to take the AN/APS-50 radar which was never actually installed.

The first short-nosed F11F-1s were delivered to VX-3 based at NAS Atlantic City, New Jersey, in February of 1957. In service, the Tiger served on the US carriers USS *Ranger*, *Intrepid*, *Saratoga*, *Forrestal* and *Bon Homme Richard*.

The Vought Crusader entered Navy service at about the same time as the Tiger and was much faster at altitude. Although easy to maintain, and having pleasant flying qualities, the Tiger was, however, plagued more by engine problems than anything else. Consequently, the US Navy became disenchanted with the Tiger and cancelled contracts for additional machines. Only around 200 F11F-1s were built before production ended with the delivery of the last F11F-1 on January 23, 1959.

The last US Navy Tigers were phased out by April 1961 after only four years of service. Following its withdrawal from fleet service, the Tiger was used primarily as a training aircraft and was retired by VT-26 in mid-1967.

The Tiger was, however, famous as the mount of the Blue Angels US Navy flight demonstration team who operated the type from April 1957 until 1969. During this time, in 1962, the F11F-1 had been redesignated F-11A.

In 1973, two ex-Blue Angels F-11As were taken from 'boneyard' storage at Davis Monthan Air Force Base and were modified by Grumman as testbeds to evaluate inflight control systems. These were the last Tigers to fly and returned to storage in 1975.

LEFT: **The Tiger was swiftly relegated to secondary duties because its performance was inferior to the much more capable and reliable Vought F-8 Crusader and the J65 engine proved unreliable and given to exploding. Note the four Sidewinder missiles under the wings of this Tiger.** ABOVE: **The Tiger's teeth. This publicity shot shows the array of weaponry with which a Tiger could be armed, including cannon, Sidewinder air-to-air missiles and unguided folding-fin rockets.** BELOW LEFT: **A fine example of 'showboating'. Despite the short front-line career, the Tiger was flown by the US Navy's Blue Angels flight team from 1957 to 1969.**

Grumman F11F-1

First flight: July 30, 1954
Power: Wright 3,379kg/7,450lb thrust J65-W-18 turbojet
Armament: Four 20mm cannon and four AIM9 Sidewinder AAMs under wings
Size: Wingspan – 9.64m/31ft 7.5in
Length – 14.31m/46ft 11.25in
Height – 4.03m/13ft 2.75in
Wing area – 23.23m²/250sq ft
Weights: Empty – 6,091kg/13,428lb
Maximum take-off – 10,052kg/22,160lb
Performance: Maximum speed – 1,207kph/750mph
Ceiling – 12,770m/41,900ft
Range – 2,044km/1,270 miles
Climb – 1,565m/5,130ft per minute

LEFT: **Apart from its powerful engines, the slender Tigercat possessed a low frontal area. The combination bestowed an impressive performance on the Grumman fighter.**
ABOVE: **Inside the pilot's 'office' of an F7F-3P photo-reconnaissance version. The funnel and hose is the pilot's 'relief tube'.**

Grumman F7F Tigercat

The Tigercat had its origins in 1941, when Grumman began design work on a hard-hitting, high-performance twin-engine fighter to operate from the Midway class of US aircraft carriers. As it developed, it was apparent that the type was going to be heavier and faster than all previous US carrier aircraft. It was also unusual for the time in that it had a tricycle undercarriage although it retained the usual arrester hook and folding wings for carrier operations.

Even before the prototype flew in December 1943, the US Marine Corps had placed an order for 500 of the F7F-1 version. They wanted to use the Tigercat primarily as a land-based fighter operating in close support of Marines on the ground. Although deliveries began in April 1944, the big Grumman fighter arrived too late to be cleared for combat use in World War II.

Wartime production had diversified to deliver the F7F-2N night-fighter, which differed from the F7F-1 by the removal of a fuel tank to make way for a radar operator cockpit and the removal of nose armament for the fitting of the radar.

An improved fighter-bomber version was also developed, the F7F-3, which had different engines for more power at altitude, a slightly larger fin and bigger fuel tanks.

Tigercat production continued after the war's end with F7F-3N and F7F-4N night-fighters, both having lengthened noses to house the latest radar – some of these aircraft were strengthened and equipped for carrier operations. Some F7F-3s were also modified for electronic and photographic reconnaissance missions.

Although it missed action in World War II, the Tigercat did see combat with the Marine Corps over Korea. USMC fighter unit VMF(N)-513 was based in Japan when the Korean War broke out. Equipped with Tigercat night-fighters, they went in to action immediately as night-intruders and performed valuable service.

The US Marines were the only military operators of the Tigercat.

ABOVE: **After their military career, a handful of Tigercats were used for water-bombing forest fires, while others were optimized for air-racing.**

Grumman F7F-3N

First flight: December 1943 (F7F-1)
Power: Two Pratt & Whitney 2,100hp R-2800-34W Double Wasp radial piston engines
Armament: Four 20mm cannon in wing roots
Size: Wingspan – 15.7m/51ft 6in
Length – 13.8m/45ft 4in
Height – 5.06m/16ft 7in
Wing area – 42.27m²/455sq ft
Weights: Empty – 7,379kg/16,270lb
Maximum take-off – 11,666kg/25,720lb
Performance: Maximum speed – 700kph/435mph
Ceiling – 1,2414m/40,700ft
Range – 1,609km/1,000 miles
Climb – 1,380m/4,530ft per minute

Grumman Tracker

The Grumman G-89 Tracker was a purpose-designed Cold War carrier-borne anti-submarine warfare aircraft that flew for the first time in December 1952. It was built to detect and then destroy fast, quiet deep-diving Soviet nuclear submarines. The aircraft would use both passive and active acoustic search systems, magnetic anomaly detection and powerful searchlights to find the enemy craft. The aircraft could work alone or with helicopters using dipping sonar to complement the Tracker's own sonobuoys. Once located, the enemy sub would be attacked with depth charges, torpedoes, bombs and rockets. Incredibly, one version of the Tracker was capable of carrying a nuclear depth charge.

The Tracker was a large high-wing monoplane with twin Wright Cyclone radial engines. Prototypes and early production aircraft were ordered at the same time in 1950, such was the need to get the type in service and keep Soviet subs in check. The type first entered service in February 1954 – although its early S2F designation was later dropped in favour of just S-2, the aircraft was popularly known as the 'Stoof' (S-two-F) throughout its career. Six military versions from S-2A to S-2G entered service.

The last Trackers in US service were eventually replaced in use by the S-3 Viking in 1976. Trackers, however, continued in service with other naval

air arms for many years. The Royal Australian Navy continued to use Trackers as front-line ASW aircraft until the mid-1980s. The Argentine Navy received its first S-2A models in the 1960s and upgraded these aircraft in the 1990s with turboprop engines.

Grumman produced 1,185 Trackers in the US and a further 99 aircraft designated CS2F were built in Canada under licence by de Havilland Canada for Canadian military use. Other customers for the Tracker included Australia, Holland, Italy, Peru, Japan, Taiwan, Venezuela, Turkey, South Korea, Thailand, Uruguay and Argentina.

From the late 1980s a number of retired US and Canadian Trackers were converted into fire-fighting aircraft called Firecats (or Turbo Firecats for the turboprop-equipped aircraft). Carrying between 800 and 1,200 US gallons of retardant in a tank replacing the military torpedo bay, these aircraft are expected to be in service in North America for years to come.

TOP: **The Tracker could carry torpedoes, depth charges and rockets – versions of the 'Stoof' in US Navy service could even carry a nuclear depth charge.** ABOVE: **A turboprop-powered remanufactured Turbo Firecat of the California Department of Forestry and Fire Protection.**

Grumman S-2E Tracker

First flight: December 4, 1952 (XS2F-1 prototype)

Power: Two Wright 1,525hp R-1820-82WA radial engines

Armament: One nuclear depth charge or homing torpedoes, depth charges or mines in weapons bay plus up to 60 sounding depth charges and 32 sonobuoys carried in the fuselage or the engine nacelles, plus a variety of bombs, rockets or torpedoes carried on underwing hardpoints

Size: Wingspan – 22.12m/72ft 7in
Length – 13.26m/43ft 6in
Height – 5.33m/17ft 6in
Wing area – 45.06m²/485sq ft

Weights: Empty – 8,310kg/18,315lb
Maximum take-off – 11,860kg/26,147lb

Performance: Maximum speed – 450kph/280mph
Ceiling – 6,700m/22,000ft
Range – 2,170km/1,350 miles
Climb – 425m/1,390ft per minute

LEFT: **An E-2C about to catch the wire on the USS *Enterprise*. The distinctive swirl painted on the aircraft's rotodome tells us this aircraft is from VAW-123 'The Screwtops'.** ABOVE: **The C-2A Greyhound is an E-2 derivative that serves in the carrier-borne delivery role. The C-2A has the same tail and wings as the Hawkeye, but has a widened fuselage with a rear-loading ramp.** BELOW: **A French Hawkeye with its carrier, *Charles de Gaulle*.**

Grumman/Northrop Grumman E-2 Hawkeye

The twin turboprop E-2 Hawkeye is the US Navy's current all-weather, carrier-based tactical battle management airborne early warning, command and control aircraft. Having a crew of five, the high-wing aircraft can be most readily identified by the 7.32m/24ft-diameter radar rotodome attached to the upper fuselage containing a radar scanner that rotates several times per minute.

At a unit cost estimated to be $80 million (75 per cent of that being electronics), the Hawkeye provides all-weather airborne early warning, airborne battle management and command and control functions for the US Carrier Strike Group. In addition the E-2 can coordinate surface surveillance and air interdiction, offensive and defensive counter air control, close air support and strike coordination, search-and-rescue airborne coordination and communications relay. An integral component of each US Navy Carrier Strike Group air wing, the E-2C uses computerized radar, Identification Friend or Foe (IFF) and electronic surveillance sensors to provide early warning threat analysis against potentially hostile air and surface targets.

The E-2 Hawkeye was the world's first carrier-based aircraft designed from scratch for the all-weather airborne early warning and command and control mission. Since replacing the Grumman E-1 in 1964, the Hawkeye has been the eyes of the US Fleet. Since its combat debut during the Vietnam War, the E-2 has served the US Navy around the world. E-2s from VAW-123 aboard the USS *America* directed F-14 Tomcat fighters flying combat air patrol during Operation 'El Dorado Canyon', the two-carrier battle group joint strike against terrorist-related Libyan targets in 1986. In the early 1990s, E-2s provided airborne command and control for Coalition air operations during the first Gulf War. Directing both strike and combat air patrol missions over Iraq, in the early days of the conflict the E-2 Hawkeye provided air control for the shoot-down of two Iraqi MIG-21 aircraft by carrier-based F/A-18. Later during the 1990s, E-2s supported Operations 'Northern' and 'Southern Watch' over Iraq. E-2s also supported NATO operations over the former Republic of Yugoslavia, including Operation 'Deny Flight'. More recently, E-2s have been widely used in Operations 'Enduring Freedom' and 'Iraqi Freedom', directing air strikes.

LEFT: **The E-2 Hawkeye is not a small aircraft, and has a wingspan of around 25m/80ft. It is one of the few military aircraft to carry a large radar dome, so it is easy to identify from most angles. Also note the four tail fins.** ABOVE: **The United States Navy quoted the unit cost of each aircraft to be $80 million.** BELOW LEFT: **The E-2 remains a vital aircraft in the US Navy inventory and will be in service for many years to come.**

The original E-2C, known as the Group 0, became operational in 1973 and has been through numerous upgrades since then. The first of these was the E-2C Group I which replaced the older APS-125 radar and T56-A-425 engines with the improved APS-139 radar and T56-A-427. This version was soon followed by the further improved Group II which featured the APS-145 radar. The Group II has been gradually upgraded with new navigation systems, displays and computers culminating in the E-2C Hawkeye 2000 variant. The latest version can track 2,000 targets simultaneously – while at the same time, detecting a further mind-boggling 20,000 targets – to a range in excess of 650km/400 miles while simultaneously guiding up to 100 air interceptions.

The E-2D Advanced Hawkeye (AHE), the newest variant of the E-2, is currently in development and is scheduled to be introduced to the US Fleet in 2011. AHE will feature a state-of-the-art advanced radar and upgraded aircraft systems that will reduce maintenance time and increase readiness. According to the US Navy, this version will "exhibit improved battle space target detection and situational awareness, support of Theater Air and Missile Defense (TAMD) operations and improved Operational Availability. The AHE mission will be to provide advance warning of approaching enemy surface units, cruise missiles and aircraft, to vector interceptors or strike aircraft to attack, and to provide area surveillance, intercept, communications relay, search and rescue, strike and air traffic control."

Variants of the E-2C Hawkeye are also flown by the Egyptian Air Force, Japanese Self Defence Air Force, Republic of Singapore Air Force, Taiwan Air Force and the French Navy.

Grumman/Northrop Grumman E-2C Hawkeye

First flight: October 21, 1960 (prototype)
Power: Two Allison 5,100ehp T56-A-425 or -427 turboprops
Armament: None
Size: Wingspan – 24.58m/80ft 7in
Length – 17.6m/57ft 9in
Height – 5.58m/18ft 4in
Wing area – 65m²/700sq ft
Weights: Empty – 17,090kg/37,678lb
Maximum take-off – 24,950kg/55,000lb
Performance: Maximum speed – 604kph/375mph
Ceiling – 9,390m/30,800ft
Range – 2,583km/1,605 miles
Climb – 766m/2,515ft per minute

Hawker Sea Fury

The Hawker Fury, inspired and influenced by a captured Focke-Wulf Fw 190, was essentially a lighter, smaller version of the Hawker Tempest. A joint 1943 British Air Ministry and Admiralty specification for a fighter/naval interceptor was written around the project. The land-based Fury first flew in September 1944, but at the war's end the RAF interest in Hawker's ultimate piston-engined fighter ceased. Development of the Sea Fury did, however, continue following the naval version's test flight in February 1945. This aircraft was essentially a navalized land plane, complete with non-folding wings. The second prototype Sea Fury was a fully navalized aircraft with folding wings and an arrester hook, and was powered by a Bristol Centaurus XV.

The production naval version, the Sea Fury Mk X, began to replace Fleet Air Arm Supermarine Seafires in service from August 1947. Meanwhile trials with external stores and RATO (rocket-assisted take-off) equipment led to the development of the Sea Fury FB. Mk 11. It was this aircraft that represented the ultimate development of British piston-engined fighters and the FB.11 proved itself to be an extremely capable combat aircraft. FAA Sea Furies were among the few British aircraft types that saw combat during the Korean War (1950–53) where they were mainly used in the ground-attack role operating from HMS *Theseus*, HMS *Ocean*, HMS *Glory* and HMAS *Sydney*. Korea was the first true jet-versus-jet war but the Sea Fury is known to have destroyed more Communist aircraft than any other non-US type and even shot down a number of North Korean MiGs.

While flying a Sea Fury off HMS *Ocean*, Royal Navy Lieutenant Peter Carmichael destroyed a MiG-15 jet and earned himself a place in the history books. "At dawn on

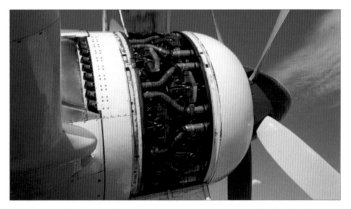

TOP: **The Sea Fury was widely exported and customers included the Royal Australian Navy who operated 101 examples the type from 1949 to 1962. As the principal fleet defence fighter of the RAN, the type flew off the aircraft carriers HMAS** Sydney **and HMAS** Vengeance. ABOVE: **Beneath the cowling, the Sea Fury's mighty Bristol Centaurus radial engine. This excellent engine was first run in July 1938 but was not properly employed for almost four years.**

August 9, 1952, I was leading a section of four aircraft on a patrol near Chinnampo. We were flying at 3,500 feet, looking for rail targets when my Number Two called out 'MiGs five o'clock – coming in!' Eight came at us from the sun. One came at me head on and I saw his tracer coming over. I managed to fire a burst and then he flashed past. I looked over my shoulder and saw an aircraft going down. When all my section called in, I knew I'd bagged a MiG! I believe the Sea Fury is the finest single-seat piston fighter ever built."

The Sea Fury, the last piston-engined fighter in RN front-line service, flew on with Royal Navy Volunteer Reserve units until 1957 and was replaced in FAA service by the jet-powered Sea Hawk.

Although the RAF rejected the Fury design, a little-known contract with Iraq saw 55 land-based Furies and five two-seat trainers delivered to the Iraqi Air Force between 1948 and 1955. The IAF are known to have used the aircraft in the counter-insurgency role. Pakistan also received Furies and used them in action against India until 1973.

Sea Furies were also exported to Egypt, Burma, Canada, Australia and the Netherlands where a number were also licence-built by Fokker. At the time of the Cuban Missile Crisis in 1962, Cuba's fighter defence centred on 15 FB.11s imported during the Batista period.

ABOVE: **Sixty examples of the Sea Fury T. Mk 20 were also produced. These were two-seat tandem trainers with two canopies connected by a Perspex 'tunnel'. The instructor, seated to the rear, could observe the student through a periscope.**
LEFT: **A preserved Sea Fury sporting the D-Day style 'invasion stripes' applied to Royal Navy aircraft during the Korean War. Note the arrester hook.**

After their military service a number of these high-performance piston aircraft were snapped up for air racing in the United States where they set world record speeds. A number remain in flying condition on both sides of the Atlantic.

ABOVE: **On the leading edge of the Sea Fury wing from left to right are two 20mm cannon muzzles (same on far right), a carburettor air intake starboard and port, and the oil cooler air intake.**

Hawker Sea Fury FB.11

First flight: September 1, 1944 (Fury)
Power: Bristol 2,480hp Centaurus 18 two-row sleeve-valve radial engine
Armament: Four 20mm cannon in outer wings plus underwing provision for up to 907kg/2,000lb of bombs or rockets
Size: Wingspan – 11.69m/38ft 4.75in (4.9m/16ft 1in folded)
Length – 10.56m/34ft 8in
Height – 4.81m/15ft 10in
Wing area – 26.01m²/280sq ft
Weights: Empty – 4,190kg/9,237lb
Maximum take-off – 5,669kg/12,500lb
Performance: Maximum speed – 740kph/460mph
Ceiling – 10,970m/36,000ft
Range – 1,223km/760 miles
Climb – 1,317m/4,320ft per minute

LEFT: **The Seasprite proved to be so capable it was put back into manufacture for the United States Navy.** ABOVE: **The continued upgrade of an essentially 1960s design with 1990s avionics has not been without problems, and in March 2008, the Australian Government cancelled its overrunning contract for SH-2Gs.**

Kaman SH-2 Seasprite

This helicopter originally entered US Navy service as the Kaman HU2K-1 having first flown on July 2, 1959. It was a single-engine helicopter primarily deployed aboard aircraft carriers in the search-and-rescue role. Redesignated UH-2A in 1962, by the end of 1965 the US Navy had received 190 single-engine UH-2A/B utility and rescue versions, most of which were upgraded during the late 1960s and 1970s. A second General Electric-built T58 turboshaft engine, an uprated transmission and a four-blade rotor gave the helicopter substantially increased load-capability and survivability.

The Seasprite was ultimately developed for the United States Navy as a ship-based fighting helicopter with anti-submarine and anti-surface threat capability. The late 1960s' Light Airborne Multi-Purpose System (LAMPS) gave the Seasprite a whole new career. LAMPS centred around the use of a light helicopter to extend the horizon of a warship's sensors and weapons – the Seasprites would track submarines

and attack them with torpedoes, and, in the anti-ship missile-defence role, provide warning of cruise missile attack. LAMPS Seasprites, designated SH-2Ds, were equipped with a search radar, an Electronic Surveillance Measures (ESM) receiver, sonobuoys, torpedoes, an active sonar repeater and a UHF acoustic data-relay transmitter. Secondary missions included medical evacuation, search and rescue, personnel and cargo transfer, as well as small boat interdiction, amphibious assault air support, gun fire spotting, mine detection and battle damage assessment.

The Seasprite SH-2F version had more powerful engines, improved rotors, a towed Magnetic Anomaly Detector (MAD), avionics upgrades, and a tailwheel moved forward to allow operations from smaller ship decks. The SH-2F was even ordered back into production after a 16-year gap, an extremely rare occurrence in aviation history. From 1982, Kaman built 54 brand new SH-2Fs for the US Navy. This

version's operational use included Operation 'Desert Storm' in 1991. The SH-2F was retired from active service in October 1993, after years of hard work. By the time of its retirement, the type was reported to need 30 hours of maintenance for each flight hour – the highest of any aircraft in the US Navy at the time.

The SH-2G Super Seasprite was a remanufactured SH-2F with much greater electronic warfare capability and more powerful engines that gave the type the highest power-to-weight ratio of any maritime helicopter. The type joined the US Navy Reserve inventory in February 1993 and was retired from service in May 2001 but currently remains in use with air arms in Egypt, Poland, Australia and New Zealand.

Kaman Seasprite

First flight: July 2, 1959 (HU2K-1)

Power: Two General Electric 1,723shp T700-GE-401 turboshafts

Armament: Torpedoes, depth charges, anti-ship or anti-tank missiles, air-to-ground missiles or unguided rockets dependent on mission

Size: Rotor diameter – 13.5m/44ft
Length – 16m/52ft 6in
Height – 4.57m/15ft

Weights: Empty – 3,447kg/7,600lb
Maximum take-off – 6,124kg/13,500lb

Performance: Maximum speed – 256kph/159mph
Service ceiling – 6,218m/20,400ft
Range – 1,000km/620 miles
Climb – 632m/2,070ft per minute

LEFT: **The Seasprite was used as a search and rescue aircraft throughout the whole Vietnam War. Between 1963 and 1964 the US Army acquired a version designated UH-2 and evaluated its ground support capabilities.**

Kamov Ka-25

The Ka-25 (NATO designation 'Hormone') was developed to meet the specification of a 1957 Soviet Navy requirement for a shipborne anti-submarine warfare helicopter. In response, Kamov developed the Ka-20 which flew for the first time during 1961 and was the basis for the production Ka-25. Around 460 were produced between 1966 and 1975 during which time the type replaced the Mil Mi-4 as the Soviet Navy's primary shipborne helicopter for killing submarines.

The Ka-25 is one of the easiest helicopters to identify thanks to Kamov's trademark counter-rotating coaxial main rotors, which dispense with the need for a tail rotor. This means the aircraft needs the shortest of tails which saves much needed space during carrier operations. Other distinguishing features include a search radar mounted beneath the nose. Though usually flown unarmed, some

ABOVE: **As well as the large search radar beneath the cockpit, versions of the Ka-25 were equipped with dipping sonar. Note the trademark counter-rotating coaxial main rotors.**

service aircraft were fitted with an internal weapons bay that could carry two torpedoes or depth charges, including nuclear versions for submarine destroying.

Up to 18 Ka-25 variants are believed to have been built, but the major sub-types were the Ka-25PL (NATO Hormone-A), the Ka-25Ts (Hormone-B, used for the guidance and targeting of

ship-launched missiles), the Ka-25PS (Hormone-C, used for SAR) and the Ka-25BShZ. The Ka-25B was the principal anti-submarine variant and was replaced in Russian service by the Ka-27. The Ka-25BShZ was developed to tow mine-sweeping equipment through the ocean.

Kamov Ka-25

First flight: 1961
Power: Two GTD-3F 900hp turboshaft engines
Armament: Torpedoes, conventional or nuclear depth charges
Size: Rotor diameter – 15.75m/51ft 8in
Length – 9.75m/32ft
Height – 5.4m/17ft 8in
Weights: Empty – 4,765kg/10,505lb
Maximum take-off – 7,200kg/15,873lb
Performance: Maximum speed – 220kph/136mph
Ceiling – 3,500m/11,483ft
Range – 400km/248 miles

Kamov Ka-27

Kamov began work on a successor for its Ka-25 in 1967, following requests from the Soviet Navy for a helicopter capable of operating night or day and in all weathers. The Ka-27 (NATO codename 'Helix') was an all-new helicopter of similar dimensions to the Ka-25 and featuring Kamov's distinctive counter-rotating coaxial main rotors. The more powerfully engined Ka-27 flew for the first time in 1973 and it is still the

Russian Navy's standard ship-based anti-submarine helicopter.

The standard Ka-27PL anti-submarine version features a search radar mounted under the nose, dipping sonar and disposable sonobuoys and was designed to operate in pairs with one tracking the enemy craft while the following helicopter dropped depth charges. A simpler version, the Ka-28, was exported to India while other

operators of the Ka-27 include Ukraine, Vietnam, South Korea and China.

A civil version of the Ka-27, the Ka-32 exists and though none has been sold to military operators, some Ka-32s in Aeroflot markings have been seen operating off Russian naval ships.

LEFT: **Retaining many of the distinctive features of the earlier Ka-25, design work on the Ka-27 began in 1967. It remains in widespread use today. It has the distinctive Kamov coaxial rotors and twin-fin tailplane of earlier models.**

Kamov Ka-27PL

First flight: 1973
Power: Two Klimov 2,205shp TV3-117V turboshaft engines
Armament: Torpedoes or depth charges
Size: Rotor diameter – 15.90m/52ft 2in
Length – 12.25m/40ft 2in
Height – 5.4m/17ft 8in
Weights: Empty – 6,100kg/13,450lb
Maximum take-off – 12,600kg/27,780lb
Performance: Maximum speed – 250kph/155mph
Ceiling – 5,000m/16,405ft
Range – 800km/496 miles
Climb – 750m/2,460ft per minute

Lockheed S-3 Viking

The versatility of the Viking has led it to be known as the 'Swiss army knife of naval aviation'. The S-3 Viking in service today is an all-weather, carrier-based patrol/attack aircraft, which provides protection for the US fleet against hostile surface vessels while also functioning as the Carrier Battle Groups' primary tanker. The S-3, one of the most successful of all carrier aircraft, is extremely versatile and is equipped for many missions, including day/night surveillance, electronic countermeasures, command and control, and communications warfare, as well as Search-And-Rescue (SAR), a vital naval role.

In the late 1960s the deployment of Soviet deep-diving nuclear-powered submarines caused the US Navy to call for a new breed of carrier-borne US Navy ASW aircraft to succeed the Grumman S-2. Lockheed, in association with Vought Aeronautics, proposed the S-3A which came to be called Viking.

To keep the aircraft aerodynamically clean, as many protuberances as possible were designed to retract so as not to reduce the aircraft's top speed. Thus, the inflight refuelling probe, the Magnetic Anomaly Detection (MAD) boom at the rear of the aircraft and some sensors retracted for transit flight. The small four-man aircraft has folding wings, making it very popular on carriers due to the small amount of space it takes up relative to the importance of its mission. With its short stubby wings, the Viking was something of a wolf in sheep's clothing and could have given a very good account of itself had the Cold War heated up. Carrying state-of-the art radar systems and extensive sonobuoy deployment and control capability, the S-3A entered US Navy service with VS-41 in February 1974. In total, 187 were built and equipped 14 US Navy squadrons.

ABOVE: **This aircraft is pictured when it served with VS-35 the 'Sea Wolves' who were described simply as a 'sea control squadron'. Note the way the Viking's wings fold unopposed for maximum space saving.**
BELOW: **The aircraft's two General Electric turbofans can keep the Viking and its crew aloft for over 3,700km/2,300 miles.**

In the mid-1980s the aircraft were completely refurbished and modified to carry the Harpoon missile, the improved version being designated the S-3B. While the S-3A was primarily configured for anti-submarine warfare, the S-3B has evolved into a premier surveillance and precision-targeting platform for the US Navy and has the most modern precision-guided missile capabilities. It does so many things so well – surface and undersea warfare, mine warfare, electronic

reconnaissance and analysis, over-the-horizon targeting, missile attack, and aerial tanking – that its current mission is summed up by the US Navy as being simply 'Sea Control'.

The S-3B's high-speed computer system processes and displays information generated by its targeting-sensor systems. To engage and destroy targets, the S-3B Viking employs an impressive array of airborne weaponry including the AGM-84 Harpoon anti-ship missile, AGM-65 Maverick infrared missile and a wide selection of conventional bombs and torpedoes. Future Viking aircraft will also have a control capability for the AGM-84 Standoff Land-Attack Missile Extended Range (SLAM-ER) missile. The S-3B provides the fleet with a very effective fixed wing, 'over the horizon' aircraft to combat the significant and varied threats presented by modern maritime combatants.

ABOVE: **The Viking has two underwing hardpoints that can be used to carry fuel tanks, general purpose and cluster bombs, missiles, rockets, and storage pods and a 'buddy' refuelling store as in the example shown. Its internal bomb bay stations can carry bombs, torpedoes and special stores.**

On March 25, 2003, an S-3B from the 'Red Griffins' of Sea Control Squadron Thirty-Eight (VS-38) became the first such aircraft to attack inland and to fire a laser-guided Maverick missile in combat. The attack was made on a 'significant naval target' in the Tigris River near Basra, Iraq. VS-38 was embarked on the USS *Constellation*.

One of the most important aircraft in the US inventory, the Viking has proved easy to update with the latest avionics and surveillance equipment. No date has been fixed for its retirement.

ABOVE: **This Viking is fitted for 'buddy' refuelling. The store under the port wing has a drogue which, when let out in flight, is used to pass fuel via the receiving aircraft's probe.**

Lockheed S-3B Viking

First flight: January 21, 1972
Power: Two General Electric 4212kg/9,275lb thrust TF-34-GE-400B turbofan engines
Armament: Up to 1,781kg/3,95lb of ordnance, including AGM-84 Harpoon, AGM-65 Maverick and AGM-84 SLAM missiles, torpedoes, rockets and bombs
Size: Wingspan – 20.93m/68ft 8in
Length – 16.26m/53ft 4in
Height – 6.93m/22ft 9in
Wing area – 55.55m²/598sq ft
Weights: Empty – 12,088kg/26,650lb
Maximum take-off – 23,831kg/52,539lb
Performance: Maximum speed – 834kph/518mph
Ceiling – 12,190m/40,000ft
Range – 3,706km/2,303 miles
Climb – 1,280m/4,200ft per minute

LEFT: **This aircraft was both the X-35A and X-35B. Following its A model testing, it was converted to B standard and had a shaft-driven lift fan fitted that amplifies engine thrust and reduces temperature and velocity during STOVL operations.**
ABOVE: **Pictured on July 7, 2006, the day the Lockheed Martin F-35 Joint Strike Fighter was officially named Lightning II.**

Lockheed Martin F-35 Lightning II

Although the US military's current first-line aircraft remain formidable weapons, their basic designs are decades old, and in the early 1990s a competition was launched to find a more modern aircraft, a Joint Strike Fighter (JSF) to fit their future needs. The two shortlisted designs came from Boeing (the X-32) and Lockheed Martin, whose X-35 was announced as the winner in October 2001. The US Air Force, the US Navy, the US Marine Corps, as well as the Royal Navy and RAF have all committed to buy what is now known as the F-35 Lightning II, the most powerful single-engine fighter in history, to replace the F-16, F/A-18 Hornet, the Harrier, Sea Harrier and the A-10.

The United States and eight international partners are involved in the F-35's funding and development. As well as the UK, Italy, the Netherlands, Turkey, Canada, Australia, Denmark

ABOVE: **The prototype X-35C carrier version first flew in December 2000. In July 2003 the historic aircraft was officially presented to the Patuxent River Naval Air Museum. The X-35B is preserved in the US by the Smithsonian.**

and Norway are also partners in the programme. Planned production is expected to exceed 3,000, making the F-35 the F-4 of the 21st century. Lockheed Martin is developing the F-35 Lightning II with its principal industrial partners, Northrop Grumman and the UK's BAE SYSTEMS. Two separate, interchangeable F-35 engines are under development: the Pratt & Whitney F135 and the GE Rolls-Royce Fighter Engine Team F136.

First flight of the Lockheed Martin X-35A conventional variant prototype was on October 24, 2000, while the first flight of the X-35C carrier variant took place on December 16, 2000. First flight of the X-35B STOVL variant prototype was in March 2001, with vertical flight testing beginning in June 2001. The first pre-production F-35 took to the air on December 15, 2006, initiating what the manufacturers described as the most comprehensive flight test programme in military aviation history. Three versions of the F-35 are under development: a Conventional Take-Off and Landing (CTOL) variant, a Short Take-Off/Vertical Landing (STOVL) variant for operating off small ships and near front-line combat zones, and a Carrier Variant (CV) for catapult launches and arrested recoveries on board US Navy aircraft carriers.

The F-35B variant, developed for the US Marine Corps, the Royal Air Force and Royal Navy, has a STOVL capability through a shaft-driven lift fan propulsion system. Other than this propulsion system, this variant only differs from the USAF F-35A conventional variant in a few details. The B model has a refuelling probe fitted into the right side of the forward fuselage, rather than the standard US Air Force refuelling receptacle usually located on the aircraft's upper surface. The STOVL variant carries no internal gun, although an external gun pack is an option. The B model shares all the electronic equipment of the USAF variant, and has a virtually identical cockpit layout except for a lever to enable the pilot to switch between hovering and flying modes. The STOVL variant, primarily designed to replace the AV-8B Harrier, has more than twice the Harrier's range on internal fuel, operates at supersonic speeds and can carry weapons internally.

The F-35C is the dedicated US Navy version and most of the differences between the F-35C and the other variants are due to its operation from full-size aircraft carriers. Accordingly the F-35C, the US Navy's first stealth aircraft, has larger wing and tail control surfaces to better manage low-speed carrier approaches. The internal structure of this variant is strengthened to handle the loads associated with catapult launches and arrested landings. The increased wingspan also provides increased range. Like the B model, the F-35C carries a refuelling probe on the right side of the forward fuselage. Weapon loads, cockpit layout, countermeasures, radar, and other features are common with the other F-35 variants but the F-35C's range and payload are superior to the strike fighters it will replace in US Navy service.

Commonality and flexibility are the basis for the F-35 design from the mission systems and subsystems to the airframe. More than 80 per cent of all parts – including the largest and most expensive components, such as the engine and key avionics units – are common on all three variants. The high degree of commonality among the variants of the F-35 and across the total development and production programme is a key to affordability.

A fully integrated weapon system allows F-35 pilots to positively identify and precisely strike mobile and moving targets in high-threat environments, day or night, in all weathers. The F-35 weapon system gives the pilot true multi-role, multi-mission capability.

F-35s are expected to be in service by 2013, and production is expected to last until around 2030.

ABOVE: **The F-35C will be the world's first stealth naval fighter, and the manufacturers state that the aircraft will be able to "endure extreme abuse without degrading its stealth radar-signature performance" on carrier decks.**
BELOW: **The first flight of the Conventional Take-Off and Landing (CTOL) F-35A version took place on December 15, 2006.**

ABOVE: **Although the F-35B can hover like a Harrier, thanks to the computers on board, in terms of pilot workload it is comparatively much easier to fly. The Lightning II will be easier for pilots to learn to fly and to maintain their currency. Compared to the Harrier, now an old design, the F-35's range is also better, the weapons load larger, and the aircraft generally much stealthier.**

Lockheed Martin F-35C Lightning II

First flight: December 16, 2000 (X-35C)
Power: One Pratt & Whitney 15,897kg/35,000lb thrust F135 turbofan
Armament: One external 25mm GAU-12 gun pod, four hardpoints in two internal weapon bays plus six external hardpoints carrying up to 7,710kg/ 17,000lb of air-to-air and air-to-ground missiles or guided munitions
Size: Wingspan – 13.1m/43ft (9.1m/29ft 10in folded)
    Length – 15.5m/50ft 10in
    Height – 4.7m/15ft 6in
    Wing area – 57.6m²/620sq ft
Weights: Empty – 10,885kg/24,000lb
    Maximum take-off – 22,680kg/50,000lb
Performance: Maximum speed – Mach 1.5 plus
    Ceiling – Unknown
    Range – 3,000km/1,863 miles
    Climb – Unknown

Martin P5M Marlin

The Martin P5M Marlin (redesignated P-5 Marlin in 1962) was a twin-engined piston-powered flying boat that entered US Navy service in 1951 and served into the late 1960s. It was developed from the company's earlier Mariner flying boat and the XP5M-1 prototype was developed from the last unfinished PBM-5 Mariner. The Mariner's wing and upper hull were married to an all-new lower hull structure and while the Marlin and the Mariner had almost identical cockpits, the Marlin had better engines – Wright R-3350 radials – and a conventional tail. It was a gull-wing aircraft with the engines and propellers kept as far away from the surface of the water as possible. The aircraft had a long hull that rose very gradually towards the tail – with greater contact with the water

the aircraft was less likely to 'porpoise' as it travelled over the water's surface.

The first flight took place in May 1948 and the first of 167 production P5M-1 aircraft appeared in 1949. Changes from the prototype included a raised flight deck for improved visibility, a large radome for the AN/APS-44 search radar in place of the nose turret, the deletion of the dorsal turret, and new, streamlined wing floats. Service deliveries began in 1952.

The P5M-1 was followed into service by 116 P5M-2 versions that had a T-shaped tail, an AN/ASQ-8 MAD boom at the rear of the tail, no tail guns, improved crew accommodation and a refined bow to reduce spray during take-off and landing. United States Coast Guard versions used for air-sea rescue were

designated P5M-1Gs and P5M-2Gs – these machines were later passed on to the US Navy.

The French Navy took delivery of ten ex-US Navy Marlins in 1959 to replace their Short Sunderlands for maritime patrol duties, operating from Dakar, Senegal, in West Africa. These Marlins were returned to the US when France withdrew from NATO.

US Navy Marlins performed coastal patrols in the Vietnam War but were largely out of service by 1965. The last official US Navy Marlin flight was in 1967 and the type was the last flying boat to see US Navy service. A P-5 is preserved at the US Naval Aviation Museum in Pensacola, Florida.

ABOVE: **The Marlin was very well armed. In addition to torpedoes, mines and even nuclear depth charges, the type was also tested with underwing rocket launchers.** LEFT: **Lacking the distinctive T-tail of the later P5M-2, the P5M-1 had a large but conventional tail. The nose housed the AN/APS-44 search radar.**

Martin P5M-2

First flight: May 30, 1948 (XP5M-1)

Power: Two Wright 3,450hp R-3350-32WA radial engines

Armament: Up to 3,629kg/8,000lb of bombs, torpedoes, mines and depth charges, including the Mk 90 nuclear depth charge

Size: Wingspan – 36.02m/118ft 2in
Length – 30.66m/100ft 7in
Height – 9.97m/32ft 8.5in
Wing area – 130.63m²/1,406sq ft

Weights: Empty – 22,900kg/50,485lb
Maximum take-off – 38,560kg/85,000lb

Performance: Maximum speed – 404kph/251mph
Ceiling – 7,315m/24,000ft
Range – 3,300km/2,050 miles
Climb – 365m/1,200ft per minute

McDonnell F2H Banshee

The F2H Banshee, though similar in design and appearance to the company's earlier FH-1 Phantom, was larger and had more powerful twin Westinghouse J34 engines which gave about twice the power of the J30 engines in the FH-1.

Designed to meet the US Navy's exacting requirements for carrier operations, while also satisfying the requirement for high speed and increased rates of climb, the F2H Banshee first flew in January 1947. It became the Navy's standard long-range all-weather fighter and entered US Navy service in 1948 as their second carrier jet fighter, after the FH-1. They served with distinction with the US Navy in Korea from 1950–53 but by the end of the conflict had been superseded by more

ABOVE: **The Banshee had unswept wings and was powered by two low-power early jet engines. The Banshee was, however, one of the USN's primary single-seat fighters during the Korean War.**

advanced designs. That said, Banshees remained in service with US Navy reserve units until the mid-1960s.

**McDonnell
F2H-3 Banshee**

First flight: January 11, 1947
Power: Two Westinghouse 1,474kg/3,250lb thrust J34-WE-34 turbojets
Armament: Four 20mm cannon plus underwing racks for 454kg/1,000lb of bombs
Size: Wingspan – 12.73m/41ft 9in
Length – 14.68m/48ft 2in
Height – 4.42m/14ft 6in
Wing area – 27.31m²/294sq ft
Weights: Empty – 5,980kg/13,183lb
Maximum take-off – 11,437kg/25,214lb
Performance: Maximum speed – 933kph/580mph
Ceiling – 14,205m/46,600ft
Range – 1,883km/1,170 miles
Climb – 2,743m/9,000ft per minute

The Royal Canadian Navy acquired 39 ex-US Navy Banshees between 1955 and 1958, operating them from shore bases and from the carrier HMCS *Bonaventure*. The Banshee was the RCN's last fighter and was not replaced when the type was retired in 1962. A total of 805 F2H Banshees were made.

McDonnell F3H Demon

The F3H Demon was the first swept-wing jet fighter aircraft built by McDonnell Aircraft and also the first aircraft designed to be armed only with missiles rather than guns. The carrier-based, transonic, all-weather Demon fighter was designed with the philosophy that carrier-based fighters need not be inferior to land-based fighters. However, the planned powerplant, the new and disappointing J40 turbojet, failed to meet

expectations and left early Demons (designated F3H-1N) underpowered. Production delays were also caused by the US Navy's desire for the Demon to be an all-weather night-fighter. And so, although the prototype had flown in August 1951, the radar-equipped Demon did not enter service until almost five years later in March 1956 as the F3H-2N and then with the Allison J71 turbojet as powerplant.

By the time production ceased in 1959, 519 Demons had been built including the definitive Demon fighter-bomber (F3H-2). At its peak US Navy use, the Demon equipped 11 front-line squadrons.

**McDonnell
F3H-2 Demon**

First flight: August 7, 1951 (XF3H-1)
Power: Allison 6,350kg/14,000lb afterburning thrust J71-A-2E turbojet
Armament: Four 20mm cannon and four AIM-7C Sparrow AAMs
Size: Wingspan – 10.77m/35ft 4in
Length – 17.96m/58ft 11in
Height – 4.44m/14ft 7in
Wing area – 48.22m²/519sq ft
Weights: Empty – 10,039kg/22,133lb
Maximum take-off – 15,377kg/33,900lb
Performance: Maximum speed – 1,041kph/647mph
Ceiling – 13,000m/42,650ft
Range – 2,205km/1,370 miles
Climb – 3,660m/12,000ft per minute

ABOVE: **The excellent visibility from its cockpit earned the Demon the nickname 'The Chair'.**

McDonnell Douglas A-4 Skyhawk

An impressive total of 2,960 Skyhawks were built from 1954 by Douglas (and later McDonnell Douglas) in a production run that lasted a quarter of a century. Designed as a small and cost-effective lightweight carrier-borne high-speed bomber, the Skyhawk was affectionately nicknamed 'the scooter' or 'Heinemann's Hot Rod' after the Douglas designer Ed Heinemann. He had been working on a compact jet-powered attack aircraft design which the US Navy ordered for evaluation – this was the XA4D-1 and the first of nine prototypes and development aircraft flew in June 1954. Development progressed quickly and the Cold War US Navy were eager to acquire this new and very capable combat aircraft. Chosen as a replacement for the venerable Skyraider, the Skyhawk provided the US Navy, US Marines Corps and 'friendly' nations with a manoeuvrable and powerful attack bomber that had great altitude and range performance as well as a remarkable and flexible weapons-carrying capability.

Production deliveries of A-4As began in September 1956. The A-4 was first delivered to the US Navy's VA-72 attack squadron on October 26, 1956. Its small size allowed it to fit on an aircraft carrier lift without needing to have folding wings

thus saving time, weight and extra maintenance. The Skyhawk was roughly half the empty weight of its contemporaries and could fly at 1089kph/677mph at sea level. Significantly, the US examples were nuclear capable.

The Skyhawk was progressively developed with more powerful engines – early A-C models had been powered by the Wright J65, a licence-built copy of the British Armstrong Siddeley Sapphire engine. The A-4C was followed by the A-4E, a heavier aircraft powered by Pratt & Whitney's J52 engine. The A-4F was the last version to enter US Navy service and was easily identified by its dorsal avionics 'hump'. The ultimate development of the Skyhawk was the A-4M, known as the Skyhawk II, specifically designed for the US Marines. This model, which first took to the air in 1970, had a larger canopy for better pilot view and had a maximum take-off weight twice that of the early A-4. Power for this 'super' Skyhawk came from a J52-P-408 and the Skyhawk II remained in production until 1979. The US Navy's Blue Angels flight demonstration aerobatics team flew the A-4 Skyhawk II from 1974 to 1986.

The Skyhawk's combat career began on August 4, 1964, with the first American carrier-launched raids on North Vietnam.

ABOVE: **Note the long front undercarriage leg of this A-4, required for carrier operations.** LEFT: **A TA-4J of training wing TW-3 from the auxiliary aircraft landing training ship USS Lexington (AVT-16). The Lexington was first commissioned on February 17, 1944, then in 1963 became a training carrier until being decommissioned in 1991.**

The A-4s were soon performing most of the Navy's and Marine Corps' light air attack missions over South-east Asia.

Skyhawks were also operated by the armed forces of Argentina, Australia, Israel (who used them extensively in the 1973 Yom Kippur war), Kuwait, Singapore, Indonesia, Malaysia and New Zealand, and they remained active with several air services into the 2000s.

Argentina was the first export customer for the Skyhawk, operating A-4Ps and A-4Qs which were modified B and C models respectively. These aircraft, acquired in the mid-1960s, were later complemented by A-4Rs which were ex-USMC A-4Ms. Argentine Skyhawks were the most destructive strike aircraft to engage British Forces during the 1982 Falklands War. Operating from mainland bases, the Skyhawks carried out many attacks against British shipping. On May 12 a Skyhawk raid put HMS *Glasgow* out of action, and on May 21 the Skyhawks attacked the British invasion force landing at San Carlos. On May 25, Argentine Skyhawks attacked and sank HMS *Coventry*. The cost of these actions was high with Argentina losing ten A-4s in a matter of days to anti-aircraft defences and the British Sea Harriers.

ABOVE: **The type was widely exported and even the example that served with the US military often masqueraded as foreign 'bogies' during aggressor training.**

LEFT: **Perhaps the best-known exported examples were those supplied to Argentina, who were the first foreign customers for the type. Flying from mainland Argentina and tanking en route, some of these A-4s were a formidable enemy during the Falklands War.**

McDonnell Douglas A-4M Skyhawk II

First flight: June 22, 1954 (XA4D-1 prototype)
Power: One Pratt & Whitney 5,081kg/11,187lb thrust J52-P-408 turbojet
Armament: Two 20mm cannon in wing roots plus up to 4,155kg/9,155lb of bombs or air-to-surface and air-to-air missiles
Size: Wingspan – 8.38m/27ft 6in
Length – 12.27m/40ft 4in
Height – 4.57m/15ft
Wing area – 24.2m²/260sq ft
Weights: Empty – 4,747kg/10,465lb
Maximum take-off – 11,115kg/24,500lb
Performance: Maximum speed – 1,100kph/683mph
Ceiling – 11,800m/38,700ft
Range – 1,480km/920 miles
Climb – 3,142m/10,300ft per minute

McDonnell Douglas F-4 Phantom II

The F-4, one of the world's greatest-ever combat aircraft, was designed to meet a US Navy requirement for a fleet defence fighter to replace the F3H Demon and to counter the threat from long-range Soviet bombers. The US Air Force also ordered the Phantom when the F-4 was shown to be faster than their high-performance F-104. The F-4 was first used by the United States Navy as an interceptor but was soon employed by the US Marine Corps in the ground attack role. Its outstanding versatility made it the first US multi-service aircraft flying with the US Air Force, Navy and Marine Corps concurrently. The remarkable Phantom excelled in air superiority, close air support, interception, air defence suppression, long-range strike, fleet defence, attack and reconnaissance.

The sophisticated F-4 was, without direction from surface-based radar, able to detect and destroy a target Beyond Visual Range (BVR). In the Vietnam and Gulf Wars alone, the F-4 was credited with 280 air-to-air victories. As a bomber the

ABOVE: **For many, the ultimate carrier-borne fighting aircraft was the F-4 Phantom II. Its versatility, performance and punch raised the bar for all combat aircraft designers.** LEFT: **F-4Js of VF-96, 'The Fighting Falcons'. This unit saw a lot of combat during the Vietnam War.**

F-4 could carry up to five tons of ordnance and deliver it accurately while flying at supersonic speeds at very low level.

Capable of flying at twice the speed of sound with ease, the Phantom was loved by its crews who considered it a workhorse that could be relied on, that could do the job and get them home safely. F-4s have also set world records for altitude (30,040m/98,556ft on December 6, 1959), speed (2,585kph/1,606mph on November 22, 1961) and a low-altitude speed record of 1,452kph/902mph that stood for 16 years.

Phantom production ran from 1958 to 1979, resulting in 5,195 aircraft. A total of 5,057 were made in St Louis, Missouri, in the US, while a further 138 were built under licence by the Mitsubishi Aircraft Co. in Japan. F-4 production peaked in 1967, when the McDonnell plant was producing 72 Phantoms per month.

ABOVE: **The 'NH' tail code tells us this is an F-4 of VF-114 'Aardvarks', pictured while operating from USS Kitty Hawk. Between 1961 and 1976 VF-114 undertook five combat cruises to take part in the Vietnam War, gaining five MiG kills in the process.**

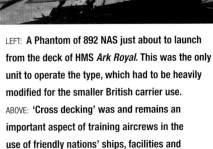

LEFT: **A Phantom of 892 NAS just about to launch from the deck of HMS Ark Royal. This was the only unit to operate the type, which had to be heavily modified for the smaller British carrier use.**
ABOVE: **'Cross decking' was and remains an important aspect of training aircrews in the use of friendly nations' ships, facilities and operating techniques.**

The USAF acquired 2,874 while the US Navy and Marine Corps operated 1,264. The F-4 was used extensively by the US in Vietnam from 1965 and served in many roles, including fighter, ground attack and reconnaissance. A number of refurbished ex-US forces aircraft were operated by other nations, including the UK, who bought a squadron of mothballed ex-US Navy F-4Js to complement the Royal Air Force's F-4Ms.

Regularly updated with the addition of state-of-the-art weaponry and radar, the Phantom served with 11 more nations around the globe – Australia, Egypt, Germany, Greece, Iran, Israel, Japan, South Korea, Spain, Turkey and the UK.

Britain's Royal Navy operated Phantoms from 1968 until 1978, mainly as a fleet defence fighter but with a secondary close support and attack role for which it was equipped to deliver nuclear weaponry. However, only one front-line Fleet Air Arm unit, No.892 Squadron aboard HMS Ark Royal, was equipped with the Phantom. The Royal Air Force also operated Phantoms from 1968 with the last RAF Phantoms being retired in January 1992.

The year 1996 saw the Phantom's retirement from US military forces by which time the type had flown more than 27,350,000km (around 17 million miles) in the nation's service. Israel, Japan, Germany, Turkey, Greece, Korea and Egypt have undertaken or plan to upgrade their F-4s and keep them flying until 2015, nearly 60 years after the Phantom's first flight.

In 2007 almost 100 Phantoms converted into unmanned QF-4 drones and missile targets were still serving the United States Navy and Air Force, and more than 800 F-4 Phantom II aircraft remained on active duty with the air arms of Egypt, Germany, Greece, Israel, Japan, South Korea, Spain and Turkey. The F-4 is one of the finest-ever combat aircraft.

ABOVE: **Showing signs of wear and tear, this F-4 is pictured on one of its many missions over Vietnam. As well as being used in that conflict by the United States Navy, the US Marine Corps and the US Air Force particularly made extensive use of the type on a variety of missions.**

McDonnell Douglas Phantom F.G.R.2 (F-4M)

First flight: February 17, 1967
Power: Two Rolls-Royce 9,305kg/20,515lb afterburning thrust Spey 202 turbofans
Armament: Eleven 454kg/1,000lb free fall or retarded conventional or nuclear bombs, 126 68mm armour-piercing rockets, one 20mm cannon, all carried externally
Size: Wingspan – 11.68m/38ft 4in
Length – 17.73m/58ft 2in
Height – 4.95m/16ft 3in
Wing area – 49.25m²/530sq ft
Weights: Empty – 14,060kg/31,000lb
Maximum take-off – 26,310kg/58,000lb
Performance: Maximum speed – 2,230kph/1,386mph
Ceiling – 18,290m/60,000ft
Range – 2,815km/1,750 miles
Climb – 9,754m/32,000ft per minute

LEFT: **The MiG-29K – a potent naval fighter.**

ABOVE: **The naval MiG's nose undercarriage is able to steer through 90 degrees each way and houses a three-colour lamp which indicates the aircraft's position on the glide path and its landing speed to a visual landing signal officer.**

Mikoyan-Gurevich MiG-29K

Over 1,200 examples of the very capable, incredibly agile MiG-29 fighter have been built and the type has been exported widely. The type was developed in the early 1970s as a high-performance, highly manoeuvrable lightweight fighter to outperform the best the West could offer. The prototype took to the air for the first time in 1977 but it was a further seven years before the type entered service – ultimately 460 were in Russian service and the rest were exported.

Codenamed 'Fulcrum' by NATO, the aircraft has been exported to Bulgaria, Germany, Cuba, Romania, Poland, Slovakia, Peru, Syria, Hungary, Iraq, India, Iran, North Korea, Malaysia and Moldova among others. It is not widely known, but the US acquired 21 MiG-29s in 1997 from Moldova after Iran had expressed interest in the high-performance fighters. In a unique accord between the US and Moldova, the aircraft were dismantled and shipped to the US.

The MiG 29's radar can track ten targets up to 245km/ 152 miles away and bestows look-down-shoot-down capability, while the pilot's helmet-mounted sight allows him or her to direct air-to-air missiles wherever the pilot looks.

The MiG is also designed for rough-field operations – special doors seal off the main air intakes to protect against foreign object ingestion during start up and taxiing. Air is drawn in via louvres in the wingroots instead and as the aircraft takes off, the inlet doors open.

The Russians have upgraded some MiG-29s to MiG-29SMT standard by increasing range and payload, replacing cockpit instruments with new monitors, and improving radar and inflight refuelling capability. Daimler Chrysler Aerospace modified a number of Polish MiGs for NATO compatibility after that nation's joining NATO in 1999 just as they did the East German MiG-29s after German reunification.

A navalized version, the MiG-29K with folding wings, fin and radome, was developed but the plans were shelved until the Indian Navy ordered the 'K' to operate from its carrier *Vikramaditya* (formerly the Russian *Admiral Gorshkov*). A $740 million contract was signed in January 2004 to supply the Indian Navy with 16 carrier-based MiG-29K/KUB aircraft (12 single-seat 'K' variants and four dual-seat 'KUB' trainers). The cost also included all training hardware including simulators.

ABOVE: **The arrester hook is fitted with lights to indicate when it is lowered. The design had to be considerably strengthened for carrier use.**

ABOVE: **A Luftwaffe land-based MiG-29 fires an AA-10 Alamo missile. The MiG-29 family equips many of the world's air forces.**

LEFT: **The aircraft's two Klimov RD-33MK turbofans have smokeless combustors, an anti-corrosive coating to cope with carrier use and a total service life of 4,000 hours with a basic overhaul time of 1,000 hours.** BELOW: **On November 1, 1989, test pilot Toktar Aubakirov carried out the first landing of a MiG-29K on the aircraft carrier *Tbilisi* that was later renamed *Admiral Kuznetsov*.**

The Indian Navy has expressed an interest in having a total of 40 MiG-29Ks. In April 2005 the Indian Navy announced that the MiG-29K's shore base will be INS *Hansa* in Goa and that the unit cost of the aircraft was $32 million. The Indian Navy received the first of its MiG-29Ks in 2007, ahead of the delivery of the carrier INS *Vikramaditya* in 2008 to allow for aircrew and ground crew training.

The export version of the MiG-29K is based on the MiG-29K airframe, but differs in a number of ways. It is lighter and cheaper, partly due to the deletion of high-cost welded aluminium lithium fuel tanks. The export MiG's fuel tanks are located in the dorsal spine fairing and wing leading-edge root extensions which affords a range increase of 50 per cent compared to land-based versions – this can be extended further by the use of the retractable refuelling probe in the port forward fuselage. The MiG-29K take-off run from a 'ski jump' carrier deck is between 125–195m/410–640ft. Extensive use of radar-absorbing materials have reduced the fighter's radar signature by up to a factor of five compared to the standard MiG-29. MiG also developed new anti-corrosion measures to protect the K's

airframe, avionics and engines. The MiG-29K can carry a wide range of weapons including 8 types of air-to-air missiles and 25 air-to-surface weapons on up to 13 hardpoints.

The dual-seat 'KUB' trainer handles almost the same as the single-seat version and the forward nose sections are identical, equipped with similar avionics and able to carry the same armament. In addition to carrying out its primary training role, the trainer has a fully operational capability.

Mikoyan-Gurevich MiG-29K

First flight: October 7, 1977 (MiG-29)

Power: Two Klimov 9,011kg/19,870lb afterburning thrust RD-33MK turbofans

Armament: One 30mm cannon, up to 13 hardpoints carrying up to 5,500kg/12,125lb of weapons, including air-to-air and air-to-surface missiles, rockets or bombs

Size: Wingspan – 11.4m/37ft 5in
Length – 14.87m/48ft 9in
Height – 4.7m/15ft 5in
Wing area – 38m²/409sq ft

Weights: Normal take-off – 18,550kg/40,895lb
Maximum take-off – 22,400kg/49,383lb

Performance: Maximum speed – 2,400kph/1,491mph
Ceiling – 27,000m/88,580ft
Range – 3,500km/2,174 miles with inflight refuelling
Climb – 17,760m/58,260ft per minute

ABOVE: **'312 Blue', one of the MiG-29K prototypes, pictured with some of the weaponry it can carry. Note the folded wingtips and extended airbrake forward of the tail as well as the extended refuelling probe.**

LEFT: **It was the sea-going Fury that led the way for the land-based Sabre, and it first flew in September 1946.** BELOW: **The swept-wing FJ-2 bore little resemblance to the earlier FJ-1.**

North American FJ Fury

Commonly thought to be a derivative of the famous F-86 Sabre, it was in fact the Fury's initial design that led to the land-based Sabre. In late 1944, the US Navy ordered a number of carrier-based jet fighters that were to be available to take part in the invasion of Japan planned for May 1946 – one of these was a North American design, the NA-134. It was a conventional straight-winged aircraft to be powered by a General Electric J35 axial-flow turbojet fed by a nose intake and having a straight-through exhaust pipe in the tail.

The USAF ordered a land-based version of the Fury designated XP-86. With the benefit of German aerodynamic research data captured at the end of World War II, the XP-86 was redesigned to incorporate swept-tail surfaces and a swept wing which would allow supersonic speeds. The naval aircraft, however, had to retain good low-speed handling capabilities for landings aboard carriers of the time so the US Navy opted to retain the straight-winged design and North American produced three prototypes of the XFJ-1 Fury.

The first XFJ-1 flew on September 11, 1946 (almost a year ahead of the more complex XP-86), and 30 production FJ-1s

were delivered from October 1947 to April 1948. The first and the only US Navy unit to receive the FJ-1 Fury was VF-5A, based at Naval Air Station North Island near San Diego in California. The first Fury deck landing took place on March 16, 1948, aboard USS *Boxer* and the aircraft was shown to be able to take off from the ship under its own power – these trials were the US Navy's first operational jet landings and take-offs at sea. Slow acceleration by these early jets during take-off led to catapulting becoming standard procedure and the greatly increased fuel consumption of the US Navy's new jet fighters demanded increased fuel storage aboard their carriers. Although the aircraft set records, its performance suffered at maximum weight and the pilots were less than impressed with its lack of cockpit temperature control.

The US Navy were aware that swept-wing fighters were essential if their jet fighters were to be a viable defence or threat, as the jet fighter dogfighting in Korea was to prove. In November 1951, the USN issued a contract for prototypes of a navalized F-86E (the FJ-2) complete with arrester hooks, lengthened nosegear (for high angle of attack carrier take-offs and landings) and catapulting capability. Trials of two XFJ-2s, powered by J47-GE-13 engines, began mid-1952. As the Korean War was drawing to a close, production of only 200 of an original order for 300 FJ-2s was undertaken at North American's newly opened Columbus, Ohio, plant. The first aircraft was delivered in October, 1952 and production continued until September 1954. By the time production began, the FJ-2 Fury was, in effect, the US Navy equivalent of the F-86F. Powered by a 2,720kg/6,000lb thrust J47-GE-2 (USN version of the J47-GE-27), the FJ-2 had folding wings, an all-moving tail for increased manoeuvrability, and was armed

LEFT: **One of the XFJ-2 prototypes undergoing carrier qualification trials in December 1952 aboard the USS *Coral Sea*. The tests exposed significant shortcomings, but the US Navy persevered.**

with four 20mm cannon each with 600 rounds. Naval equipment took the take-off weight up to 8530kg/18,810lb compared with 8080kg/17,810lb for the F-86F.

The first squadron to receive FJ-2s was Marine VMF-122 at Cherry Point, North Carolina, in January 1954, followed five months later by VMF-235 aboard USS *Hancock*, a carrier recently equipped with new C-11 steam catapults. By 1955 FJ-2s equipped six Marine squadrons, three with the Atlantic Fleet, and three with the Pacific Fleet.

In March 1952, North American had begun design of the FJ-3 Fury powered by the Wright J65-W-2 Sapphire, built under licence from Britain's Armstrong Siddeley. This version went on to equip 12 US Navy squadrons and on August 22, 1955, an FJ-3 flown by Commander R.G. Dose became the first American aircraft to use the mirror landing system that soon became standard throughout USN carriers. Late-build FJs were equipped to carry Sidewinder heat-seeking missiles. When FJ-3 production ended in August 1956, the US Navy and Marines were operating 23 Fury squadrons.

In the FJ-4 the entire airframe was revised. A thinner wing of greater area and span was used and the addition of a dorsal spine from cockpit to fin makes this version easy to identify. Classified as long-range attack fighters, the FJ-4 carried additional armour in the nose while drop tanks, bombs or Sidewinders could be carried under the wings. The first FJ-4s to enter service joined Marine Squadron VMF-451 in 1956, and by March 1957 152 aircraft were in the inventory.

December 4, 1956, saw the test flight of a new variant, the FJ-4B. Equivalent to the US Air Force's F-86H Sabre, the FJ-4B was fully equipped for low-altitude attack and, apart from being able to carry even more underwing stores, the aircraft could also deliver tactical nuclear weapons.

The 'Bravo Fury' carried inflight refuelling probes beneath the port wing, and in June 1957 'buddy' refuelling was introduced. By the addition of underwing fuel packs, the Fury could take on enough fuel from another Fury to extend its combat radius by around 50 per cent. In October 1958, this technique was used

ABOVE: **The US Navy were slow to adopt swept-wing designs for carrier operations due to required lower stalling speeds and better low-speed handling characteristics. This is why the Navy stuck with straight-wing fighter designs long after the USAF had moved on to swept-wing designs for their front-line fighters. Korean conflicts with faster MiGs persuaded the US Navy they had to change.** BELOW: **Furies went on to equip USMC squadrons too.**

by Marine Squadrons VMA-212 and 214 to complete the first trans-Pacific crossing by single-seat naval aircraft.

Although by the early 1960s Furies were being phased out of the front line, their work was done – from conventional beginnings the Fury helped the US Navy keep pace with fighter technology. In all, North American's Columbus plant delivered 1,112 Furies to the US military.

ABOVE: **From 1962 the FJ-4 was designated the F-1E, and the FJ-4B became the AF-1E. A total of 1,115 Furies were received by the US Navy and Marine Corps – an impressive production run.**

North American Fury FJ-3

First flight: September 11, 1946 (XFJ-1)
Power: Wright 3,497kg/7,700lb afterburning thrust J65-W-2 turbojet
Armament: Four 20mm cannon
Size: Wingspan – 11.3m/37ft 1in
　　　Length – 11.3m/37ft 1in
　　　Height – 4.17m/13.8ft
　　　Wing area – 26.75m²/288sq ft
Weights: Empty – 5,535kg/12,205lb
　　　Maximum take-off – 8,573kg/18,900lb
Performance: Maximum speed – 1,096kph/681mph
　　　Ceiling – 14,934m/49,000ft
　　　Range – 1,593km/990 miles
　　　Climb – 2,577m/8,450ft per minute

LEFT: **The reconnaissance mission of the modified Vigilantes served the US Navy well during the Vietnam War and beyond. This RA-5C flew from USS *Ranger*.** ABOVE: **Another RA-5C, this time on the deck of the *Forrestal*.**

North American A3J/A-5 Vigilante

In November 1953, North American Aviation began work on a design project for an all-weather long-range carrier-based strike aircraft capable of delivering a nuclear weapon at speeds of up to Mach 2. To meet the needs of the design, the team proposed an aircraft so advanced in many ways that it is fair to say that when the Vigilante appeared, no other aircraft had incorporated so many technological innovations.

The first prototype, the YA3J-1, was rolled out on May 16, 1958, and was officially named Vigilante. The first flight took place on August 31, 1958, and the aircraft went supersonic for the first time on September 5. A second prototype entered the flight test programme in November that year. The first production A3J-1s soon followed and the sixth Vigilante constructed made 14 launches and landings on the USS *Saratoga* in July 1960.

The demands made on an aircraft flying at twice the speed of sound are considerable and special measures have to be taken to ensure that systems continue to function in this very harsh environment. In the case of the Vigilante, pure nitrogen was used instead of hydraulic fluid in some of the airframe's hottest areas. The Vigilante was structurally unusual in that major elements were made of titanium to protect against aerodynamic heating while the wing skins were machined as one piece from aluminium-lithium alloy – gold plate was used as a heat reflector in the engine bays.

Advanced aerodynamic features included a small high-loaded swept wing with powerful flaps and a one-piece powered vertical tail. Revolutionary fully variable engine inlets were fitted to slow down supersonic air to subsonic speed before it reached the engine thus producing maximum performance from the engines at any speed. A fully retractable refuelling probe was built into the forward port fuselage ahead of the pilot's cockpit.

The A3J-1 Vigilante also featured some extremely advanced electronics for the time, including the first production fly-by-wire control system, although a mechanical system was retained as back-up. Bombing and navigation computations were carried out by an airborne digital computer, and the

FAR LEFT: **Vigilantes on the deck of the US Navy carrier USS *Ranger*. It was from the deck of this carrier that the last Vigilante catapult launch took place on September 21, 1979. The aircraft were all mothballed or scrapped within weeks.** LEFT: **The Vigilante was a large naval aircraft and had a unique means of delivering the nuclear store it was designed to carry. Even when the Vigilante was modified for reconnaissance duties it retained its weapon-carrying capability but was never armed.**

aircraft had the first operational Head-Up Display (HUD). The aircraft's radar had early terrain avoidance features relieving some of the pilot's workload at low-level. In December 1960 the Vigilante set a new world altitude record for its class when it carried a 1,000kg/2,403lb payload to a height of 27,893m/ 91,451ft, exceeding the then record by 6.4km/4 miles.

The Vigilante's jaw-dropping innovation reached new heights with its weapons delivery. A nuclear weapon was stored in a unique internal weapons bay without bomb bay doors in the aircraft belly and instead of the nuclear bomb being dropped, the weapon (which was mounted in a long duct that extended back between the two engines) was ejected to the rear during release. This was a complex system and prone to technical problems which kept Vigilante crews appropriately vigilant.

The first squadron deployment occurred in August 1962 aboard the USS *Enterprise* on its first cruise and in September that year, the A3J-1 was redesignated A-5A under the new US Tri-Service designation system. Shortly thereafter, the US Navy's strategic deterrent mission was assumed by nuclear-powered and nuclear missile-equipped Polaris submarines and further procurement of the A-5A was halted after only 59 had been built. Most were returned to North American for conversion to RA-5C standard – 53 were eventually rebuilt as RA-5Cs and were joined in service by 55 new production aircraft. The RA-5C retained the bomber version's very high speed performance and was capable of electromagnetic, optical, and electronic reconnaissance. The type was used to great effect by the US 7th Fleet during carrier air wing operations in the Vietnam War. The US Navy's last RA-5C fleet squadron was disbanded in September 1979.

ABOVE: **When it entered service, the Vigilante was one of the largest and by far the most complex aircraft to operate from United States Navy aircraft carriers. A total of 158 were built.**

North American A-5 Vigilante

First flight: August 31, 1958 (YA3J-1)

Power: Two General Electric 7,326kg/16,150lb afterburning thrust J79-2 turbojets

Armament: One Mk 27, Mk 28, or Mk 43 nuclear bomb in the linear weapons bay, plus one Mk 43 nuclear or a pair of Mk 83 or Mk 84 conventional bombs on weapons pylon beneath each wing

Size: Wingspan – 16.15m/53ft
Length – 23.11m/75ft 10in
Height – 5.92m/19ft 5in
Wing area – 70.05m²/754sq ft

Weights: Empty – 17,240kg/38,000lb
Maximum take-off – 36,285kg/80,000lb

Performance: Maximum speed –
2,230kph/1,385mph
Service ceiling – 20,420m/67,000ft
Range – 5,150km/3,200 miles
Climb – 2,440m/8,000ft per minute

ShinMaywa PS-1/US-1

This aircraft is a rare bird in service these days – a large four-engined (technically, five-engined) amphibian flying boat. Equally rare is the fact that the type re-entered production some years after initial production ceased.

Shin Meiwa were a rebranded Kawanishi company who, during World War II, had demonstrated the ability to build excellent flying boats – the company name later changed again to today's ShinMaywa. Although in the early 1950s Shin Meiwa simply serviced aircraft, the team's flying boat heritage

ABOVE: **In December 2003, the US-1A Kai powered by four Rolls-Royce AE 2100 turboprops completed its first flight in Kobe, Japan. A CTS800-4K engine, produced by Rolls-Royce and Honeywell, was also fitted to the aircraft to drive the boundary layer control system that provides a short take-off and landing capability.** BELOW: **A ShinMaywa PS-1 water-bomber in action.**

and skill pool was not forgotten. In 1959 the company rebuilt a Grumman UF-1 Albatross, which flew in 1960 as an aerodynamically advanced technology demonstrator flying boat, and the company was back in the flying boat business.

The Japanese Maritime Self Defence Force were impressed with the results and in January 1966 awarded a contract to develop the design into a service ASW patrol aircraft. The PS-1 was designed as a high-wing monoplane with fixed floats connected to the underside of the outer wing by struts. A retractable beaching undercarriage enabled this version to taxi on, but not land on nor take off from, land. The nose gear retracted into the hull, while the main wheels pivoted up and into the sides of the fuselage. Flight-testing of two PS-X prototypes began in October 1967 and service evaluation was carried out by the 51st Flight Test Squadron. After testing, the first prototype went on to be converted for evaluation as a firebomber aircraft by Japan's National Fire Agency.

Satisfied by the results of the PS-X programme, the JMSDF ordered the aircraft into production in 1969 as the PS-1 although its makers always knew the aircraft as the SS-2. The aircraft featured an innovative boundary layer control system powered by an independent gas turbine, a 1,400ehp Ishikawajima T-58-1H1-10 carried in the fuselage – this is a means of increasing the lift generated by wings by ejecting high-velocity engine exhaust gases over the wings and control surfaces to generate even more lift. It was this feature that gave the aircraft its good STOL capability. Other innovations

RIGHT: **Note the large nose-radar, the high-set wing and the pronounced hull shape of the flying boat. The recess for the starboard main landing gear can be seen in the fuselage just above and behind the mainwheel. Note also the red danger line painted on the side of the fuselage to warn of the spinning propeller blades.** BELOW: **This PS-1 is preserved at Kanoya Naval Air Base Museum in Japan.**

included a system to suppress spray to ensure that the engines were not flooded with sea water on landings and take-offs.

Sensor systems included search radar with the antenna in a large nose radome, a Magnetic Anomaly Detection (MAD) system with a retractable 'stinger' boom and a passive sonar system with 20 sonobuoys. The aircraft could carry two homing torpedoes each in two pods between the engines on each wing. Four 150kg/330lb depth charges could be carried internally, while wingtip pods could accommodate three 127mm/5in rockets each. No defensive armament was carried.

Twenty-three aircraft – a small, expensive and politically sensitive production run – entered service with the JMSDF between 1971 and 1978, and served until 1989 when they were replaced by the P-3 Orion.

It was not long after the ASW version had entered service that the JMSDF called for the development of a search and rescue version – this led to the US-1. With military armament, equipment and sensor systems removed, the aircraft had a much greater fuel capacity, rescue equipment and full landing gear which made the new version a true amphibian. It first flew on October 15, 1974, and the first of 19 aircraft entered service the following year. Early in production, an uprated version of the original engines was substituted but all of the earlier aircraft were modified to this US-1A standard. Over 23 years of service Japanese US-1s were used in over 500 rescues and saved 550 lives.

Funding would not permit the development of an all new aircraft to replace the aging US-1 fleet so in 1995 ShinMaywa proposed an upgraded version of the US-1A, the US-1A Kai (short for *kaizen* which means modification). This aircraft, now designated US-2, features aerodynamic refinements, more powerful engines and a pressurized hull. Flight testing began with the prototype's maiden flight from Osaka Bay on December 18, 2003.

ABOVE: **The PS-1/US-1 family of flying boats have confounded those who believed the post-war world had no place for large flying boats. Derivatives of these aircraft will be flying for years to come.**

ShinMaywa US-1A

First flight: October 4, 1967 (PX-S prototype)
Power: Four General Electric 3,493ehp T64 (Ishikawajima 10J) turboprops
Armament: None
Size: Wingspan – 33.15m/108ft 9in
Length – 33.46m/109ft 9in
Height – 9.82m/32ft 3in
Wing area – 136m²/1,463sq ft
Weights: Empty – 25,500kg/56,220lb
Maximum take-off – 45,000kg/99,200lb
Performance: Maximum speed – 495kph/310mph
Ceiling – 8,200m/26,900ft
Range – 4,200km/2,610 miles
Climb – 713m/2,340ft per minute

LEFT: **A United States Navy HO3S-1 pictured over the deck of the USS _Kearsage_. The S-51 design was widely used in many forms in Korea, and went on to serve in a variety of roles around the world.**

Sikorsky S-51/Westland Dragonfly

Sikorsky carried out ground-breaking helicopter development work in the early 1940s. Building on the success of this, the company developed the all-new VS-337, a tandem two-seater helicopter powered by a 450hp radial engine – it first flew on August 18, 1943. This design became the R-5 (later the H-5) and was ultimately widely known by Sikorsky's own designation – the S-51. This became the world's first true production military helicopter.

As helicopters became more capable and reliable so their many applications became clear. Early H-5s were fitted on each side with stretcher carriers for casualty evacuation duties and later, rescue hoists. The four-seat version of the S-51 was proposed for civil use and enabled Los Angeles Airways to launch the first scheduled helicopter mail service in October 1947.

In US Army service, the H-5 was used for spotting and communications work, but it is perhaps best known for its role as a rescue aircraft during the Korean War. It is worth pointing out that until the S-51 there was no production aircraft available to the US military that could take off and land vertically. Short take-off and landing aircraft were in use but could not land in, for example, a jungle clearing. Accordingly, the S-51 afforded the military a new means of extracting personnel from behind enemy lines or from the sea before they could be taken prisoner. The helicopter could also swiftly evacuate wounded personnel from a battlefield and so saved countless lives. Production lasted until 1951, by which time Sikorsky had built 285 machines.

In 1946, UK company Westland had negotiated what came to be a very long-standing licence agreement with Sikorsky – this led to the UK production of a Westland-built S-51 that first flew in 1948. The Dragonfly was a thorough redesign of the S-51 and not just a licence-build – 139 machines were built before production ceased in 1953.

LEFT: **Among the duties at which the S-51 proved most useful was casualty evacuation. The picture shows a USAF H-5H in Korea, 1952, with its external 'casualty pods'. The value of helicopters to the military became clear after World War II but Korea proved them in every way, especially in the rescue of downed aircrew behind enemy lines.**
ABOVE: **The Royal Navy were early adopters of the Sikorsky design but in the form of the Westland Dragonfly.**

Introducing the British Alvis Leonides engine, the Dragonfly was assembled from UK-made components and became the first UK-built helicopter in British military service. The Royal Navy was the first UK military customer with the HR. Mk 1, an air-sea rescue version powered by the Leonides 50. The first RN Dragonfly unit and indeed the service's first helicopter squadron was No.705 Naval Air Squadron formed at Royal Naval Air Station Gosport. Rescue versions of the Dragonfly were equipped with a hoist capable of lifting 170kg/375lb. The introduction of helicopters into the USN and Royal Navy was to transform the services' capabilities not just in ASR but in the ASW mission too.

The RAF's HC. Mk 2 was similar to the Royal Navy version but built for the casualty evacuation role. The Royal Navy's main ASR version was, however, the HR. Mk 3 with 58 machines built. It, like the RAF's HC. Mk 4 again built for the 'casevac' role, differed from the earlier versions mainly by the introduction of all-metal rotor blades and hydraulic servo controls.

RAF Dragonflies served in the anti-terrorist operations in Malaya from 1950 and in three and a half years these helicopters evacuated 675 casualties and carried over 4,000 passengers and 38,100kg/84,000lb of supplies in around 6,000 sorties. Royal Navy Dragonflies operated from aircraft carriers to rescue the crews of aircraft that crashed into the sea.

Proving the type's pioneering position, the world's first regular, scheduled helicopter passenger service was established by BEA (British European Airways) using the S-51 on June 1, 1950, initially between Cardiff and Liverpool.

Westland developed the five-seat Widgeon from the Dragonfly but it only saw limited production as it competed against more sophisticated second-generation helicopter designs.

In addition to operators in the US and UK, the pioneering S-51 and Dragonfly was also exported to Canada, Japan, the Philippines, Thailand, Belgium, Egypt, France, Iraq, Italy, Ceylon and Yugoslavia.

ABOVE: **Just a few years before, the pilot of this ditched F4U Corsair would have had to hope to be picked up by a friendly ship or flying boat or face capture or drowning. Rescues of aircrew downed in the sea rose dramatically thanks to this helicopter, in this case an H-5H variant.** BELOW: **Two classic Sikorsky designs, both of which were taken on by Westlands in the UK and then produced as, top, the Westland Whirlwind (Sikorsky S-55) and below, the Westland Dragonfly. WG722 was a Whirlwind HR. Mk 3.**

ABOVE: **This excellent side view of another Royal Navy HR. Mk 3 shows some of the helicopter's main recognition features including the boxy greenhouse glazed nose and the long and slender tail boom.**

Sikorsky/ Westland Dragonfly HR. Mk 1

First flight: October 5, 1948 (Westland Sikorsky WS-51 prototype)

Power: One Alvis 540hp Leonides 50 radial piston engine

Armament: None

Size: Rotor diameter – 14.63m/48ft
Length – 17.54m/57ft 6.5in
Height – 3.95m/12ft 11.5in

Weights: Empty – 1,986kg/4,380lb
Maximum take-off – 2,663kg/5,870lb

Performance: Maximum speed – 153kph/95mph
Service ceiling – 3,780m/12,400ft
Range – 483km/300 miles
Climb – 244m/800ft per minute

Sikorsky SH-60 Seahawk

The SH-60 Seahawk is a twin-engine medium-lift utility or assault helicopter. It is used for anti-submarine warfare, search-and-rescue, drug interdiction, anti-ship warfare, cargo lift and special operations.

When the US Navy issued a requirement for an updated Light Airborne Multi-Purpose System (LAMPS) helicopter to operate from smaller naval escorts, Boeing and Sikorsky each submitted proposals. Following a 1977 fly-off, the Sikorsky machine, a development of the US Army's Sikorsky UH-60A Black Hawk, was named the winner. While the Seahawk uses the same basic airframe of the UH-60A, the Seahawk is far more expensive and complex due to the addition of extensive avionics and weapons systems. The Navy received the SH-60B Seahawk in 1983.

The SH-60B Seahawk is equipped primarily for Anti-Submarine Warfare (ASW) through a complex system of sensors carried aboard the helicopter including a towed Magnetic Anomaly Detector (MAD), air-launched sonobuoys (sonic detectors) and torpedoes. The SH-60B carries out Anti-Ship Surveillance and Targeting (ASST) operating from cruisers, destroyers, and frigates and can extend the range of the ships' radar capabilities.

ABOVE LEFT: **Described by its manufacturers as the world's most capable maritime helicopter, the Seahawk was created by a team with unparalleled experience in the production of helicopters for maritime missions. With 600 Seahawks in service around the world and 2.5 million flight hours logged, the Seahawk is by any standard an outstanding naval helicopter.** ABOVE RIGHT: **A Seahawk uses its dipping sonar to listen for submarines under the watchful eye of its carrier.** BELOW LEFT: **Flying the flag – the Seahawk has already served the US Navy for over a quarter of a century.**

Other sensors include the APS-124 search radar, ALQ-142 ESM system and optional nose-mounted Forward-Looking Infra-Red (FLIR) turret. The primary means of attack is with the Mk 46 or Mk 50 torpedo, AGM-114 Hellfire missiles and the capability of a single cabin door-mounted M-60D or GAU-16 machine-gun for defence. A standard crew for a 'Bravo' model is one pilot, one ATO/Co-Pilot (Airborne Tactical Officer) and an enlisted aviation systems warfare operator (sensor operator).

Other capabilities include search and rescue, replenishment, and medical evacuation missions. Due to the success of the original SH-60B variant, the US Navy has also developed the HH-60H special operations model and the improved SH-60F carrier-borne ASW model. All US Navy models will be replaced in time by the MH-60R and MH-60S versions. The US Coast Guard also uses the HH-60J search and rescue version.

The SH-60F 'Foxtrot' is the carrier-based version of the 'Bravo'. It is the primary means of Anti-Submarine Warfare (ASW) and Search-And-Rescue (SAR) for carrier battle group commanders and exists to defend the carrier battle group. It differs from the 'Bravo' in means of submarine detection, utilizing the AQS-13F dipping sonar rather than a MAD detector and carrying fewer sonobuoys

LEFT: A Seahawk fires a sea-skimming AGM-119 Penguin anti-ship missile. Propelled by a solid rocket engine, the missile performs random weaving manoeuvres as it approaches the target and then hits close to the waterline. The delay fuse causes the warhead to detonate inside the hull of the target ship. BELOW: The twin-engine Seahawk is used for anti-submarine warfare, search and rescue, drug interdiction, anti-ship warfare, cargo lift, and special operations.

(14 rather than the 25 of the 'Bravo'). The 'Foxtrot' is capable of carrying the Mk 46 torpedo and a choice of cabin-mounted guns including the M-60D, M-240 and GAU-16 machine-guns for defence. Standard crew for a Foxtrot is one pilot, one co-pilot, one enlisted Tactical Sensor Operator (TSO) and one enlisted Acoustic Sensor Operator (ASO).

The HH-60H 'Hotel' version is the primary Combat Search-And-Rescue (CSAR), Naval Special Warfare (NSW) and Anti-Surface Warfare (ASUW) helicopter in the US Navy. It carries a variety of defensive and offensive sensors making it one of the most survivable helicopters in the world. Sensors include a FLIR turret with laser designator and the Aircraft Survival Equipment (ASE) package, including the ALQ-144 Infra-Red Jammer, AVR-2 Laser Detectors, APR-39(V)2 Radar Detectors, AAR-47 Missile Launch Detectors and ALE-47 chaff/flare dispensers. Engine exhaust deflectors provide infrared thermal reduction, limiting the threat of heat-seeking missiles. The Hotel can carry up to four AGM-114 Hellfire missiles on an extended wing using the M-299 launcher and a variety of cabin and port window-mounted guns, including M-60D, M-240, GAU-16 and GAU-17 machine-guns. Standard crew for an H model is one pilot, one co-pilot and two 'door gunner' crewmen.

The MH-60S 'Sierra' was developed after the navy decided to phase out the CH-46 Sea Knight helicopter. The 'Sierra' is deployed aboard amphibious assault ships and fast combat supply ships. It has two missions – troop transport and Vertical Replenishment (VERTREP) but can also perform Search-And-Rescue (SAR). The 'Sierra' has no offensive sensors but can carry the ALQ-199 Infra-Red Jammer. However, the Sierra is the first US Navy helicopter with a glass cockpit, in which flight data information is relayed to pilots using four digital screens rather than electromechanical gauges and dials. The primary means of defence is with the M-60D, M-240 or GAU-17, though a 'batwing' in development may be added to accommodate missiles or larger guns and cannon.

In addition to the United States Navy and US Coast Guard, Seahawks were also acquired by Australia, Greece, Japan, Spain, Taiwan, Thailand and Turkey.

LEFT: Although this SH-60 Seahawk is carrying out cargo duties, note the Forward-Looking Infra-Red (FLIR) turret mounted on the nose. The US Navy's anti-submarine screen has to be able to operate day and night in all weathers to protect the surface ships, and the FLIR makes this possible.

Sikorsky SH-60B Seahawk

First flight: December 12, 1979 (YSH-60B)

Power: Two General Electric 3,380shp T700-401 turboshafts

Armament: Air-to-surface missile AGM-84 Harpoon, AGM-114 Hellfire, AGM-119 Penguin, Sea Skua, or up to two Mk 46 or Mk 50 ASW torpedoes, Mk 36 mine, Mk 35 depth charge, sonobuoys, dipping sonar, MAD towed array

Size: Rotor diameter – 24.08m/79ft
Length – 19.76m/64ft 10in
Height – 5.8m/17ft

Weights: Empty – 6,190kg/13,650lb
Maximum take-off – 9,909kg/21,845lb

Performance: Maximum speed – 235kph/145mph
Service ceiling – 5,790m/19,000ft
Range – 805km/500 miles
Climb – 214m/700ft per minute

LEFT: **The MH-53 Sea Dragon is among the world's largest helicopters but its size hides an impressive flexibility among its special duties.**
ABOVE: **The large container attached to the port sponson is an auxiliary fuel tank that can hold up to 2,461 litres/650 US gallons of extra fuel. There is another one on the starboard side.**

Sikorsky CH-53E Sea Stallion and MH-53 family

The Sikorsky CH-53 Sea Stallion was designed to meet a 1960 US Marines requirement for a new heavy-lift assault transport. Using some systems from their earlier Skycrane, Sikorsky produced a helicopter that remains a key military asset to this day. The first prototype flew in October 1964 and production deliveries of CH-53As began in 1966 – within a year the type was in action in Vietnam. It was at that time that the USAF ordered its first combat rescue version of the CH-53, the HH-52 'Jolly Green Giant', to extract downed pilots from enemy territory.

The CH-53D was a more capable version of the CH-53A. Used extensively both afloat and ashore, the Sea Stallion was the heavy-lift helicopter for the Marine Corps until the introduction of the CH-53E triple-engine variant of the H-53 family into the fleet in 1981. The CH-53D continued in service and performed its multi-role mission lifting both equipment and personnel in training and combat, including Operation 'Desert Storm', the first Gulf War, where the helicopter performed with distinction.

Improvements to the CH-53E included the addition of a third engine to give the aircraft the ability to lift the majority of the US Marines' transportable equipment, a dual-point cargo hook system, improved main rotor blades and composite tail rotor blades. A dual digital automatic flight-control system and engine anti-ice system give the aircraft an all-weather capability.

The CH-53E Super Stallion is designed for the transportation of equipment, supplies and personnel during the assault phase of an amphibious operation and subsequent operations ashore. Capable of both internal and external transportation of supplies, the CH-53E can operate from ships in the most adverse

LEFT: **The large, unwieldy yet sophisticated MH-53J is a US Air Force helicopter that is dedicated to rescuing downed pilots and supporting US special operations troops such as the US Navy Seals.**

weather conditions, day or night. The three-engine helicopter has external range-extension fuel tanks, 'crashworthy' fuel tanks and defensive electronic countermeasure equipment. The helicopter will carry 37 passengers in its normal configuration and 55 passengers with extra seats installed. The CH-53E can carry external loads at increased airspeeds due to the stability achieved with the dual-point hook system.

The helicopter is capable of lifting 16,260kg/35,850lb at sea level, transporting the load 92.5km/57.5 miles and returning. A typical load would be a 7,250kg/16,000lb M198 howitzer or an 11,800kg/26,000lb Light Armored Vehicle (LAV). The aircraft can also retrieve downed aircraft, including another CH-53E. Equipped with a refuelling probe, the CH-53 can be refuelled in flight, giving the helicopter a technically indefinite range. However, with a typical four and a half hours' endurance, the Super Stallion can move more equipment over rugged terrain in bad weather and at night. During Operation 'Eastern Exit' in January 1990, two CH-53Es launched at sea, flew 857km/532.45 miles at night, refuelling twice en route, to rescue American and foreign allies from the American Embassy in the civil war-torn capital of Mogadishu, Somalia. It was two CH-53Es that rescued Air Force Captain Scott O'Grady following his high-profile downing over Bosnia in June 1995.

The newest military version of Sikorsky's H-53 series is the MH-53E Sea Dragon, the Western world's largest helicopter, used primarily for Airborne Mine Countermeasures (AMCM), with a secondary mission of shipboard delivery. Additional mission capabilities include air-to-air refuelling, hover inflight refuelling, search-and-rescue, and external cargo transport operations over land and at sea.

The MH-53E is heavier and has a greater fuel capacity than the CH-53E but can operate from carriers and other warships. The Sea Dragon is capable of carrying up to 55 troops or a 16,260kg/35,850lb payload but perhaps its most interesting capability is its ability to tow a variety of mine-sweeping countermeasures systems, including the Mk 105 mine-sweeping sled, the ASQ-14 side-scan sonar, and the Mk 103 mechanical mine-sweeping system.

The MH-53J version performs low-level, long-range, undetected penetration into hostile areas, day or night, in adverse weather, to drop, pick up or supply US special forces. This version is the largest and most powerful helicopter in the US Air Force inventory, and is believed to be the most technologically advanced helicopter in the world. Its terrain-following, terrain-avoidance radar and forward-looking infrared sensor, along with a projected map display, enable the crew to follow terrain contours and avoid obstacles, making low-level penetration possible at night in all weathers. The helicopter is equipped with armour plating, and a combination of three 7.62mm miniguns or 0.50 calibre machine-guns. It can transport 38 troops or 14 litters and has an external cargo hook with a 9,070kg/20,000lb capacity.

ABOVE: The MH-53E has enlarged side-mounted fuel sponsons and is configured for towing its mine-sweeping ALQ-166 hydrofoil sled for detonating magnetic mines from high above. BELOW: Some 125 examples of the CH-53D Sea Stallion were delivered to the US Marine Corps between 1969 and 1972.

BELOW: The CH-53E's seven-blade main rotor assembly is powered by three T64-GE-416 turboshaft engines. The downdraft created by the main rotors is enough have earned the CH-53E the nickname of 'the hurricane maker'. Note the protected engine air intakes and the refuelling probe.

Sikorsky CH-53E Super Stallion

First flight: October 14, 1964 (CH-53 prototype)
Power: Three General Electric 4,380shp T64-GE-416/416A turboshaft engines
Armament: Usually none
Size: Rotor diameter – 24.08m/79ft
  Length – 30.2m/99ft 1in
  Height – 8.97m/29ft 5in
Weights: Empty – 15,070kg/33,226lb
  Maximum take-off – 33,340kg/73,500lb
Performance: Maximum speed – 315kph/196mph
  Service ceiling – 5,639m/18,500ft
  Range – 925km/574 miles with 9,070kg/20,000lb external payload
  Climb – 763m/2,500ft per minute with 9,070kg/20,000lb external payload

LEFT: **Derived from the Su-27, the Su-33 differs not only in having navalized features like folding wings and an arrester hook but also by having the ability to refuel in mid-air. Note the Su-33's large canards that shorten the aircraft's take-off distance and improve manoeuvrability.**

Sukhoi Su-33

It was in 1985 that the first outline design for a navalized version of the famous Su-27 fighter was approved to provide the Soviet Navy's new carriers with an air superiority fighter for self-defence. The carrier-borne aircraft was at first designated Su-27K (K for *korabelny* or shipborne) but was later given the Su-33 designation. The NATO reporting name for the new version of the Su-27 was 'Flanker-D'.

The naval version differed from the land-based Su-27 by the addition of canards near the junction of the wing and leading edge extension for better manoeuvrability while generating more lift thereby reducing take-off runs and landing speed. Wing area was increased, although the span remained the same as its shore-based cousin, and the fins were shortened to enable the fighter to fit in the typically crowded hangars of an aircraft carrier.

The Su-33 also featured redesigned power-assisted folding outer wing panels, separately controlled aileron and flaps and an upgraded fly-by-wire control system and hydraulic system. The airframe and landing gear were also strengthened to cope with the additional stresses of carrier operations as well as being treated for improved corrosion resistance. The nose gear was changed to a twin-wheeled version with a telescopic strut and an additional landing light and three-colour indicator lights for the carrier-based flight controller's visual reference of the approaching aircraft's glide-patch and landing speed. The aircraft was, of course, also equipped with a retractable arrester-hook system. The AL-31F engines were uprated to enable the pilot to recover from a failed hook-up and aborted landing so he had enough power to go around again.

The drag chute was removed from the shortened tail boom and the horizontal stabilizers and nosecone could all fold up with the wings to reduce the aircraft's dimensions onboard ship. Another two hardpoints were added together with a retractable inflight refuelling probe on the port side of the aircraft, forward of the cockpit. The aircraft's navigation, automatic landing and fire-control systems were all upgraded to cope with the very different environment of operating from an aircraft carrier.

ABOVE: **As well as air defence, Su-33 duties were planned to include destruction of enemy ASW, AWACS and transport aircraft.** RIGHT: **The wings were fitted with power-assisted folding, and the vertical tails were shortened compared to the Su-27 to allow the fighter to fit in the hangar of an aircraft carrier. Also the Infra-Red Search and Track sensor was moved forward to provide better downward visibility.**

The Su-33 entered service with the Northern Fleet in 1994, based on the only Russian Navy carrier in service, the *Admiral Kuznetsov*, which sailed with 13 examples on board for the first time in 1995. Before embarking, each pilot made up to 400 landings on a concrete runway training deck painted to match the size and shape of the carrier deck to perfect their technique before being allowed to attempt landings at sea on a deck moving in all planes.

The training of Su-27K pilots is carried out on the Su-27 KUB. This is a combat-capable trainer fitted with a side-by-side cockpit as a tandem cockpit arrangement would not have allowed sufficient visibility for the instructor in the back seat to make a safe carrier landing. The Su-27 KUB also has a larger wing area as well as larger canards, ventral fins, rudders and horizontal stabilizers to enable lower approach speeds and safer landings. The maiden flight, first carrier landing and take-off of the Su-27 KUB all took place in 1999.

ABOVE: **Su-33s and Kamov Ka-27s on the deck of the carrier *Admiral Kuznetsov*. Commissioned in January 1991, the carrier does not have a catapult, which limits the size and weight of aircraft that can be carried.**

The Su-33 can carry a range of guided weapons, including missiles to intercept anti-ship missiles. In addition to the air defence role, the Su-33 can be tasked with the destruction of enemy ASW, AWACS and transport aircraft, anti-shipping strike and support of amphibious landings. Reconnaissance and laying of minefields are also within this very capable aircraft's remit.

Some 24 examples of the Su-33 were built and that seemed to be the end of production for the type. However, in late 2006 the Russian media revealed that talks were underway to supply up to 50 Su-33s to China to operate from the former Soviet carrier *Varyag*, acquired by China from the Ukraine in 1999.

ABOVE: **Sukhoi Su-33s operate from the *Kuznetsov* by using a forward ski-jump pioneered by the British, and then recover using arrester wires.**

Sukhoi Su-33

First flight: April 29, 1999 (Su-27KUB)

Power: Two Lyulka 12,558kg/27,690lb thrust AL-31F afterburning turbofans

Armament: One 30mm cannon and up to 6,500kg/14,330lb of ordnance on 12 external hardpoints, including air-to-air or air-to-surface missiles, bombs, rockets or ECM pods

Size: Wingspan – 14.7m/48ft 3in extended
Length – 21.94m/72ft
Height – 5.92m/19ft 6in
Wing area – 62m²/667sq ft

Weights: Empty – 16,000kg/35,275lb
Maximum take-off – 33,000kg/72,750lb

Performance: Maximum speed – 2,300kph/1,430mph
Ceiling – 17,000m/55,770ft
Range – 3,000km/1,860 miles
Climb – 13,800m/45,275ft per minute

LEFT: **The straight-winged Attacker was the Royal Navy's first jet fighter and was a 'tail dragger', unusual at a time when most designers were opting for tricycle undercarriages for jets. The use of the Spiteful's wing led to the aircraft's working name of 'Jet Spiteful' before Attacker was applied.**

Supermarine Attacker

The Supermarine Attacker was originally designed to a wartime RAF specification and combined a Nene jet engine with the laminar-flow wing (minus radiators) and landing gear of the piston-engined Spiteful. This simplified approach was taken to get another British single-seat jet fighter in service as soon as possible – the swollen fuselage lines of the Attacker were simply due to the diameter of the centrifugal-flow Nene turbojet. The second and third prototypes had different landing gear and were essentially made to demonstrate carrier capability. Trials on HMS *Illustrious* led to Royal Navy and Pakistan Air Force orders.

Although the prototype first flew in July 1946, the type did not enter service until August 1951 and then with the Royal Navy who maintained interest in the Attacker long after the RAF gave up on it.

The Fleet Air Arm took delivery of 52 Attacker F. Mk 1 interceptors, 8 FB. Mk 1 fighter-bombers (both Mk 1s powered by the Rolls-Royce Nene 3) and 82 FB. Mk 2 fighter-bombers powered by the Nene 102. The FB. Mk 1 could carry two 454kg/1,000lb bombs or four 27kg/60lb rocket projectiles as well as the standard fighter armament of four 20mm cannon. The 36 Attackers supplied to Pakistan were land-based

aircraft – they were basically Attacker Mk 1s but minus folding wings and other naval equipment. The range of the Attacker could be increased by carrying a bulbous belly tank.

The Attacker was in many ways an unremarkable aircraft and the tailwheel made deck landing difficult, but as the first Fleet Air Arm jet fighter in front-line use, the Attacker provided the Royal Navy with its first foothold in the jet age. The type was phased out of front-line use in 1954 after only three years when it was replaced by the Sea Hawk and Sea Venom. Royal Navy Volunteer Reserve (RNVR) units continued to operate the type until 1957.

ABOVE: **Due the limitations of the early jet engine that powered the Attacker it was felt that the type would not be able to fight above 10,670m/35,000ft. Two examples survive, one in Britain and one in Pakistan.**

Supermarine Attacker F. Mk 1

First flight: July 27, 1946
Power: Rolls-Royce 2,271kg/5,000lb thrust Nene 3 turbojet
Armament: Four 20mm cannon in wings
Size: Wingspan – 11.25m/36ft 11in
Length – 11.43m/37ft 6in
Height – 3.02m/9ft 11in
Wing area – 21m²/226sq ft
Weights: Empty – 3,826kg/8,434lb
Maximum take-off – 5,539kg/12,211lb
Performance: Maximum speed – 950kph/590mph
Ceiling – 13,715m/45,000ft
Range – 950km/590 miles
Climb – 1,936m/6,350ft per minute

Supermarine Scimitar

This large and heavy fighter was the Royal Navy's first swept-wing single-seat jet aircraft, the first RN aircraft equipped to carry an atomic bomb and the last fighter aircraft to bear the famous Supermarine name. Derived from the Supermarine Type 525 that first flew on April 27, 1954, the Scimitar's role evolved from a single-seat fighter to a low-level strike aircraft with nuclear capability. The first production Scimitar flew on January 11, 1957, and production Scimitars were first delivered to the Royal Navy for evaluation in August of that year.

The first front-line Scimitar unit to be formed was 803 Naval Air Squadron. After working up at RNAS Lossiemouth, the unit took part in the 1960 Farnborough SBAC show, before embarking on HMS *Victorious*. Unfortunately, 803's commanding officer was killed when his aircraft went over the side of the carrier due to a failed arrester wire – this happened in front of the press and so the Scimitar's unfortunate reputation was born.

The Scimitar was, at the time of its introduction, the heaviest and most powerful aircraft ever to serve in the Fleet Air Arm. Operating large and fast aircraft from relatively small aircraft carriers made take-offs and landings particularly hazardous. The Scimitar was designed with a tail 'bumper' on which the aircraft would rest for take-off, while the aircraft's nosewheel was high in the air, actually clear of the carrier deck. Launching with this increased angle of attack meant the catapults on the Royal Navy's carriers could still manage to launch the heavy Scimitar.

Accident rates were high – of the 76 Scimitars produced, 39 were lost in a variety of accidents. The Scimitar was, however, equally at home carrying out low-level bombing attacks, high-altitude interception with air-to-air missiles and long-range fighter reconnaissance – it was a quantum leap on from the Sea Hawk which it replaced as the Navy's standard single-seat strike fighter. Although only produced in small numbers, the Scimitars gave the Royal Navy a nuclear punch.

Mounting losses and the arrival of the Blackburn Buccaneer saw the Scimitar relegated to second-line duties. However, the early Buccaneer's underpowered engines meant that Buccaneers could not take off with a full fuel and weapons load, so Scimitars were configured to provide 'buddy' refuelling – that way the Buccaneers could take off with minimum fuel but maximum weapons load then refuel from a Scimitar immediately. Scimitars were also used as high-speed target banner tug aircraft.

The last front-line squadron (803 NAS) surrendered their Scimitars in October 1966 but the Fleet Requirements Unit flew them for testing and training purposes until the end of 1970.

TOP LEFT: **Although this large, twin-engined fighter was produced in limited numbers it served the Royal Navy well in a variety of roles for a decade.**
TOP RIGHT: **The large wing area is evident in this study of a Scimitar F.1. The dorsal spine extending forwards from the tail had an air intake at the end.**
ABOVE: **The wings' drooping leading edges and large flaps kept carrier handling of this large aircraft within essential limits.**

Supermarine Scimitar F.1

First flight: January 11, 1957
Power: Two Rolls-Royce 5,105kg/11,250lb static thrust Avon 202 turbojets
Armament: Four 30mm cannon; wing pylons for up to 96 air-to-air rockets or a range of other stores
Size: Wingspan – 11.33m/37ft 2in
Length – 16.87m/55ft 4in
Height – 5.28m/17ft 4in
Wing area – 45.06m^2/485sq ft
Weights: Empty – 10,869kg/23,962lb
Maximum take-off – 15,513kg/34,200lb
Performance: Maximum speed –
1,143kph/710mph
Ceiling – 14,020m/46,000ft
Range – 2,288km/1,422 miles
Climb – 3,660m/12,000ft per minute

Vought A-7 Corsair II

Derived from Vought's F-8 Crusader but a completely new aircraft, the single-seat A-7 Corsair II was one of the most successful modern military aircraft. At a unit cost of just over $1 million and the lowest loss rate of any US military aircraft in the Vietnam War, the A-7 gave the US taxpayer outstanding value for money. In over five million flight hours between 1968 and 1991, US Navy and Air Force A-7s were the US military's most cost-effective aerial weapon.

The A-7 resulted from a 1962 United States Navy requirement for an A-4 Skyhawk replacement with improved range and weapon-carrying capability as well as more accurate weapons delivery. The Navy insisted that to keep cost down, all proposals had to be based on existing aircraft designs so Vought's was based on the F-8 Crusader.

The pace of the project was remarkable. Vought's winning response was announced on February 11, 1964, and the YA-7A prototype first flew in September 1965, almost a month ahead

TOP: **This is a Corsair II of VA-12, Attack Squadron Twelve, which operated the A-7E from April 1971. The photo was taken when the unit was part of Carrier Attack Wing Seven.** ABOVE: **Portugal operated a number of ex-United States Navy A-7As (20) and TA-7Cs (6). Deliveries to Portugal began in May 1981, and the aircraft were finally retired in 1999.**

of schedule. By now the aircraft was called Corsair II, reprising the name of the company's famous wartime naval fighter. The first operational US Navy squadron aircraft was delivered in October 1966 and the type first saw combat in December 1967. Twenty-seven front-line US Navy units were equipped with A-7s during the Vietnam war.

The A-7 was shorter than the F-8 but had a bigger span wing, although not of the variable-incidence kind. Power came from the Pratt & Whitney TF30-P-6 turbofan developed for the F-111. The engine did not have an afterburner, as supersonic speed was not a requirement of the early A-7. This power and the fact that the aircraft was much lighter than the F-8 meant that range and weapons load were greatly increased.

The aircraft was equipped with an advanced radar that was integrated with a digital navigation system and a digital weapons computer for increased accuracy from a greater distance, thereby reducing exposure to the risks to be found nearer to targets. The Corsair II was the first US combat aircraft with the now standard head-up display, and also had a projected map display system that accurately displayed the

ABOVE: **Loaded with bombs and missiles this wing-folded A-7 was pictured on the deck of the carrier USS *John F. Kennedy* (CV-67), the last conventionally powered aircraft carrier built by the US Navy.**

aircraft's position to the pilot on two different scaled maps. Production of 199 A-7As was followed by 196 A-7Bs and 67 C models – all were basically the same aircraft but with engine updates and modifications.

As they did with the US Navy's F-4, the USAF also ordered the A-7 as a low-cost interim successor to the F-105 until the F-111 was available. The YA-7D prototype with the TF30 flew on April 6, 1968, while the first TF41-powered aircraft took to the air on September 26, 1968. The first USAF version was the A-7D with a fixed high-speed refuelling receptacle behind the cockpit to 'fit' the KC-135 tanker's flying boom instead of the folding refuelling probe of US Navy aircraft. The USAF chose the M61 Vulcan Gatling gun rather than the twin single-barrel 20mm cannon fitted in USN aircraft, and chose a different engine in the form of the Allison TF41-A-1, a licensed version of the Rolls-Royce Spey. This version also had more comprehensive avionics to enable weapons delivery in all conditions, day or night. The US Navy later adopted its own version of this model which was designated A-7E.

United States Air Force A-7Ds flew a total of 12,928 combat sorties during the Vietnam War and were second only to the mighty B-52 Stratofortress in the weight of ordnance dropped on Hanoi. The last shot fired in anger by a United States military aircraft in South-east Asia came from an A-7D of the 345th Tactical Fighter Wing operating from Korat, Thailand, on August 15, 1973.

The A-7E was the final US fleet version and could carry up to 6,800kg/15,000lb of bombs and missiles on eight weapons points. A-7E Corsair IIs were part of the two-carrier battle group that carried out strikes on Libyan terrorist-related targets in 1986. The US Navy flew its last A-7E combat missions during the 1990 Gulf War. During 'Desert Storm', the A-7 achieved 95 per cent operational readiness and did not miss a single combat sortie. The type was fully retired from USN service in 1993. This very capable aircraft became a victim of the US Department for Defense's decision to acquire stealthy,

ABOVE: **The Corsair flew on in US Navy service until 1993 after 27 years of front-line service and a formidable combat record.** BELOW: **The A-7A could carry a fraction of the weapons load later versions were cleared to fly with. Notice the two weapons carrying points under each wing and the rail on the side of the fuselage for carrying Sidewinders.**

multi-role supersonic fighter/attack aircraft that cost 50 times more at new than the single-purpose A-7.

With the exception of some used in deception tactics for the then top secret F-117 programme, most USAF A-7s were phased out by 1991.

The A-7 production line had continued until September 1984 by which time 1,545 examples had been built of which 113 were remanufactured to produce later models. A-7s were also exported to Portugal, Greece and Thailand.

ABOVE: **The Corsair II won its spurs in Vietnam where it served with both the US Navy and later the US Air Force. It is rightly considered to be one of the best ever combat aircraft.**

Vought A-7E Corsair II

First flight: September 27, 1965 (YA-7A)

Power: Allison 6577kg/14500lb thrust TF41-A-2 turbofan

Armament: One 20mm cannon and up to 6,804kg/15,000lb of missiles, rockets and bombs

Size: Wingspan – 11.81m/38ft 9in
Length – 14.06m/46ft 1.5in
Height – 4.9m/16ft 1in
Wing area – 34.84m²/375sq ft

Weights: Empty – 8,841kg/19,490lb
Maximum take-off – 19,051kg/42,000lb

Performance: Maximum speed –
1,123kph/698mph
Ceiling – 12,800m/42,000ft
Range – 2,300km/1,430 miles
Climb – 4,572m/15,000ft per minute

Vought F-8 Crusader

The Crusader single-seat naval jet fighter began as Vought's response to a 1952 US Navy requirement for a carrier-based supersonic fighter. The prototype first took to the air in March 1955 and exceeded Mach 1 during this initial flight making it the first aircraft designed for shipboard operation to fly faster than sound.

Jet aircraft carrier operations dictate that aircraft have very robust landing gear, an arrester hook and folding wings but all these features add to the overall weight of the aircraft and can compromise performance. Vought came up with a brilliant variable-incidence wing which, on take-off and landing, could be pivoted through seven degrees. This gave the wing a high angle of attack and so reduced landing approach speeds. The raised centre section of the wing also acted as a speed brake to reduce landing speed further.

Armament consisted of four 20mm cannon, two on either side of the fuselage. Behind the guns, on each side of the aircraft, was a launch rail for a single Sidewinder missile. Although the prototype did not have wing stores pylons, these came on later production models.

The first production version of the F8U-1 Crusader, as it was then named, flew at the end of September 1955, and the US Navy accepted its first operational F8U-1 on December 28, 1956. The US Navy was eager to show off their new fighter and a series of speed and endurance records were set by Crusaders in 1956–57. On July 16, 1957, an F8U-1 and an F8U-1P reconnaissance model attempted to set a coast-to-coast speed record. The pilot of the F8U-1P that landed in New York after a flight of just three hours and 23 minutes, was Major John Glenn, who was as a result a celebrity before his career as a NASA astronaut and later a US senator.

TOP: **The French Aéronavale were the main overseas customer for what was known in US fighter pilot circles as 'the last of the gunfighters' as it was the last US fighter designed with guns as its primary weapon.** ABOVE: **The F-8 was among the first supersonic fighters and remained potent for over 40 years. Notice how long the aircraft is compared to the one-man cockpit.**

The F8U-1E had an improved radar system that gave it limited all-weather capability while the more powerful F8U-2 incorporated a further improved radar and fire-control system, as well as an uprated J57-P-16 engine with 7670kg/16,900lb of afterburning thrust.

The next version was the F8U-2N, with new avionics including a push-button autopilot, and the uprated J57-P-20 engine, with increased afterburning thrust of 8,165kg/18,000lb. Yet more versions followed. The first F8U-2NE flew at the end of June 1961 and carried an improved search and fire-control radar system for enhanced all-weather operation.

In September 1962 the US Navy introduced an aircraft designation system in line with US Air Force designations, so existing Crusader variant designations were changed. The F8U-1 became the F-8A and the later models changed from F8U-1E/F-8B, F8U-2/F-8C, F8U-2N/F-8D, F8U-2NE/F-8E, F8U-1P/RF-8A.

LEFT: **The Crusader's brilliant variable-incidence wing, seen here in use ready for a carrier launch, reduced take-off and landing speeds. US Navy Crusaders were formidable dogfighters during the Vietnam air war and downed at least 18 enemy aircraft.**
ABOVE: **When an aircraft is this good, you are allowed to show off in it sometimes. The Crusader was the first carrier-based aircraft to reach a speed of 1609kmh/1000mph.**

One final new-production model was built – the F-8E(FN), built for the French Aéronavale. However, French carriers were smaller than American carriers, and this dictated new engineering including blown flaps to reduce the aircraft's landing speed.

The Aéronavale operated 42 Crusaders from the carriers *Clemenceau* and *Foch*. The French aircraft also had the capability to carry two Matra R.530 air-to-air missiles and eventually four Matra Magic R.550 heat-seeking missiles, in place of Sidewinders.

The Crusader was used by both US Marine and US Navy detachments during the war in Vietnam, its combat debut coming on August 2, 1964. North Vietnamese patrol boats attacked the US Navy destroyer *Maddox* so four Crusaders from the carrier *Ticonderoga* attacked and sank one of the

patrol boats. The Marines used the aircraft largely in the attack role, but the US Navy used the Crusader as a dogfighter and in the period 1966–68 shot down at least 18 MiGs.

The Crusader proved so effective that in 1966 a re-engineering programme was established to refurbish and improve the type. Stronger wings and main landing gear plus blown flaps (devised for the French Crusaders) were added to a total of 446 rebuilt.

By 1972, fighter versions of the F-8 Crusader were being phased out of US Navy service, but in 1978, 25 refurbished US Navy F-8Hs were sold on to the Philippine Air Force as F-8Ps – they were finally retired in 1986. The Aéronavale Crusaders were the last of the type in service and were replaced by the Rafale from 2000, bringing more than four decades of Crusader service to an end.

ABOVE: **An F-8 prepares to launch from the USS *Constellation* during Vietnam. Throughout the conflict the aircraft served in photographic, reconnaissance, strike and fighter roles.**

Vought F-8E Crusader

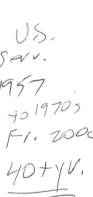

First flight: March 25, 1955
Power: Pratt & Whitney 8,165kg/18,000lb afterburning thrust J57-P-20A turbojet
Armament: Four 20mm cannon, four AIM-9 Sidewinder AAMs, or two AGM-12B Bullpup missiles
Size: Wingspan – 10.72m/35ft 2in
Length – 16.61m/54ft 6in
Height – 4.8m/15ft 9in
Wing area – 32.52m²/350sq ft
Weights: Empty – 9,038kg/19,925lb
Maximum take-off – 15,422kg/34,000lb
Performance: Maximum speed – 1,800kph/1,120mph
Ceiling – 17,983m/59,000ft
Range – 966km/600 miles
Climb – 17,374m/57,000ft in 6 minutes

Westland Lynx

A 1964 British Army requirement calling for a multi-role helicopter able to carry seven fully-armed troops, a 1,360kg/3,000lb load and operate in the casualty evacuation, reconnaissance, or liaison roles led Westland to develop a helicopter that became known as the Lynx. Westland also appreciated the Royal Navy's need for a second-generation helicopter to operate from ships in adverse weather. Meanwhile, France was also looking for an armed reconnaissance and ASW helicopter. The result was an Anglo-French agreement under which Westland would design and produce 70 per cent of a new aircraft while Aérospatiale in France produced the rest. Significantly, the Lynx was the first British aircraft designed using metric and not imperial measurements.

Following design and development, the first prototype Lynx flew in 1971. Of the 13 development machines, the first Royal Navy HAS Mk 2 version flew in 1972. It introduced a lengthened nose for a radar scanner and a wheeled undercarriage as opposed to skids. The first Lynx landing at sea took place on June 29, 1973 aboard Royal Fleet Auxiliary *Engadine*.

ABOVE LEFT: **The Royal Navy's Lynx HMA.8 is a sophisticated, versatile naval helicopter able to carry out anti-submarine, anti-surface and search and rescue missions. The Royal Navy operated HMA. 8s from all their escort ships, destroyers and frigates.** ABOVE RIGHT: **Early in its career the Lynx established itself as the world's best light naval multi-role helicopter.**

In 1972 a Lynx broke the world record over 15km/9.3 miles and 25km/15.5 miles for helicopters by flying at a speed of 321.74kph/200mph. It also set a new 100km/62-mile closed-circuit record flying at 318.504kph/198mph. In 1986 a modified Lynx piloted by John Egginton set an absolute-speed record for helicopters over a 15km/9.3-mile and 25km/15.5-mile course by reaching speeds up to 400.87kph/249.09mph. The Lynx remains one of the most agile helicopters in the world, capable of performing loops and rolls and has equipped the Royal Navy's Black Cats aerobatic display team.

The first production Lynx HAS Mk 2 flew in 1976 and deck-handling trials began on HMS *Birmingham* at sea in February 1977. The first Royal Navy Lynx squadron, No.702 NAS, was commissioned in 1978 leading to the type operating from over 40 ships, mainly frigates and destroyers. The HAS Mk 2 was developed principally for anti-submarine duties, operating from destroyers and frigates. It brought a significant capability to the Royal Navy operating in the air-to-surface search and strike, SAR, troop transport, reconnaissance, fire support, fleet liaison and communication roles. Eighty HAS2s were delivered with the final 20 receiving uprated engines – these machines were designated Mk 3. The French Aéronavale also widely deployed the type.

LEFT: **XX510 was the second naval Lynx prototype and, along with other trials machines, was subjected to tough testing to ensure the design could cope with the harsh carrier environment.**

2

LEFT: **As well as traditional anti-submarine duties, the Royal Navy's Lynx HMA.8 is used to protect British interests around the world. In 2007, a helicopter operating from RFA *Largs Bay* took parts in an anti-drugs operation in the Caribbean and helped in the seizure of £20 million worth of cocaine.** BELOW: **The French Navy is one of the other prime operators of the Lynx. Usually, naval versions have the tricycle undercarriage while army/utility versions have skids.**

About 25 Royal Navy Lynx took part in the Falklands War and their first action came on April 25, 1982, when a pair of Mk 2s attacked and helped to disable the Argentine submarine *Santa Fe*. Actions on May 3, 1982, best illustrate the capability of the Lynx. HMS *Coventry*'s Lynx launched two Sea Skua missiles at a vessel detected on radar and scored direct hits. Shortly afterwards the Lynx from HMS *Glasgow* was fired at by what it thought to be the same vessel. It launched its missiles from 14.4km/9 miles range, completely destroying the vessel's superstructure. The Navy Lynx went on to see more action in the first Gulf War when the Lynx's Sea Skua was used to devastating effect against the Iraqi Navy.

The Lynx AH.7 currently in service with the Fleet Air Arm operates as an attack/utility helicopter in support of the Royal Marines while the Lynx HMA.8 is an anti-submarine warfare helicopter equipped with the Sea Skua anti-ship missile for Royal Navy warships. The Lynx was back in action during the invasion of Iraq in 2003 – a Lynx from 847 Naval Air Squadron was shot down over Basra, Iraq on May 6, 2006.

Although the Lynx is due to be phased out of service from 2012, the sea-borne Lynx remains possibly the best small ship helicopter in the world.

On June 22, 2006, the UK Ministry of Defence awarded Westland a £1 billion contract for 70 Future Lynx helicopters, described as a new aircraft that builds on the dynamic and vehicle systems of the existing design, incorporating advanced technology and providing increased capability. Future Lynx will feature a redesigned nose and rear fuselage to give greater space and easier access to avionic units. Power will come from two LHTEC CTS800 engines, offering increased power, endurance and economy over existing Lynx powerplants. The Royal Navy variant will be in service from 2015.

As well as Britain and France, Lynx have been operated by the navies of Brazil, Norway, Denmark, Portugal, Germany, Egypt, Argentina, Nigeria, South Korea and the Netherlands.

ABOVE: **The Netherlands acquired a number of versions, including eight for anti-submarine warfare. The entire Dutch Lynx fleet was upgraded in the early 1990s, and fitted with four-bag flotation systems.**

Westland Lynx HAS 8

First flight: March 21, 1971 (prototype)
Power: Two Rolls-Royce Gem 1,135shp 42-1 turboshafts
Armament: Torpedoes, depth charges, anti-ship or anti–tank missiles, dependent on mission
Size: Rotor diameter – 12.8m/42ft
    Length – 15.24m/50ft
    Height – 3.76m/12ft 1in
Weights: Empty – 3,291kg/7,255lb
    Maximum take-off – 5,125kg/11,300lb
Performance: Maximum speed – 232kph/144mph
    Service ceiling – 2,576m/8,450ft
    Range – 275km/171 miles
    Climb – 661m/2,170ft per minute

LEFT: **Flying the flag for the Royal Navy, this Sea King HAS.6 from 816 NAS had its tiger markings applied for the annual Tiger Meet of NATO aircraft.**

ABOVE: **This shot of an 820 NAS Sea King shows a close up of one of the emergency flotation bags in its container above the starboard wheel.**

Westland (Sikorsky) Sea King

The Westland Sea King is a British licence-built version of the Sikorsky S-61 helicopter of the same name, built by Westland Helicopters, now Agusta Westland. Although the aircraft share a name, the British aircraft differs considerably from the American version by having British-built Gnome engines, British anti-submarine warfare systems and a fully computerized control system. The Westland Sea King was also developed for a much wider range of missions than the Sikorsky Sea King.

A 1969 agreement between Westland and Sikorsky allowed the British company to use the Sikorsky Sea King airframe and rotor system to meet a Royal Navy requirement for an anti-submarine warfare helicopter to replace the Westland Wessex, itself a British version of a Sikorsky machine.

The prototype and pre-production machines used Sikorsky-built components but the first Westland-built aircraft and the first production version for the Royal Navy, the Sea King HAS1,

had its maiden flight on May 7, 1969. It was delivered to the Royal Navy in the same year while the last Westland Sea King was built over 20 years later in 1990 – a lengthy production run.

The basic ASW Sea King was upgraded numerous times, becoming the HAS2, HAS5 and HAS6, which was replaced in service by the Merlin. Surviving aircraft are having their mission equipment removed and the aircraft are being used in the utility role.

A troop-carrying version, the Commando, was originally developed for the Egyptian Air Force. Capable of transporting 27 fully equipped troops over 640km/400 miles, it retained the folding rotor blades and tail of the ASW variants. This version is fitted with an external cargo hook capable of carrying underslung loads of up to 2,720kg/6,000lb such as Land Rovers and the 105mm Light Gun. A rescue hoist is fitted as standard. Designated Sea King HC. Mk 4 by the Royal Navy, it remains in service as an important asset for amphibious assaults.

LEFT: **Derived from the export Commando, the Westland Sea King HC Mk 4 is an all-weather, day and night amphibious medium support helicopter. It is cleared for operations from nearly all Royal Navy and many foreign warships, and is equally at home providing support to ground forces when ashore, in all conditions.**

A dedicated search-and-rescue version, the Sea King HAR3, was developed for the RAF, and entered service from September 1977 to replace the Westland Whirlwind and, later, the Wessex, in the search-and-rescue role. These aircraft provide 24-hour SAR cover around the UK and the Falkland Islands. SAR versions of the Sea King were also produced for the Royal Norwegian Air Force, the German Navy, and later for the Belgian Air Force.

The latest variant of the Sea King is the ASaC, formerly known as Airborne Early Warning (AEW). During the Falklands War a number of warships were lost, with casualties, due to the lack of a local AEW capability. Two HAS2 Sea Kings were hastily modified in 1982 to become the Sea King AEW2A. Thirteen Sea Kings were eventually modified, the main difference being the addition of the Thales Searchwater radar attached to the side of the fuselage on a swivelling arm and protected by an inflatable dome. The helicopter lowers the radar in flight and raises it for landing. Further modifications led to the designation AEW7 and then the ASaC7, a further upgrade of the AEW7. The main role of the ASaC Sea King is detection of low-flying attack aircraft. It also provides interception/attack control and over-the-horizon targeting for surface-launched weapon systems. The ASaC7's radar can simultaneously track 400 targets.

Royal Navy Sea Kings proved their remarkable versatility and endurance during the Falklands War of 1982, performing mainly anti-submarine search and attack, also replenishment, troop transport and Special Forces insertions into the occupied islands. During the 1991 Gulf War its roles included air-sea rescue, inter-ship transporting duties and transporting Royal Marines on to any suspect ships that refused to turn around during the enforced embargo on Iraq.

The Sea King participated in the UN's intervention in Bosnia, with Sea Kings operated by 820 Naval Air Squadron and 845 Naval Air Squadron. The Sea Kings from 820 NAS were deployed from Royal Fleet Auxiliary ships and provided logistical support, rather than the ASW role in which the squadron specialized, ferrying troops and supplies across

ABOVE: **The Airborne Surveillance and Area Control (ASaC) – previously Airborne Early Warning – Sea King was rapidly brought into Royal Navy service after the Falklands War, when it became clear that Airborne Early Warning remained an essential part of air power and survival at sea.** BELOW: **A Royal Navy Sea King lowers its dipping sonar to listen for submarines beneath the surface.**

the Adriatic Sea. They performed over 1,400 deck landings and flew in excess of 1,900 hours. The Sea Kings from 845 NAS performed vital casualty evacuation and other tasks and were hit numerous times. In NATO's intervention in Kosovo, ship-based Sea Kings from 814 NAS provided search and rescue as well as transporting troops and supplies. During the 2003 invasion of Iraq the Sea Kings provided logistical support, transporting Royal Marines from their offshore bases on *Ark Royal*, *Ocean* and other ships on to land in Kuwait. In July 2006 Sea King HC.4s from RNAS Yeovilton were deployed to Cyprus to assist with the evacuation of British citizens from Lebanon. Westland Sea Kings were also exported to Australia, Belgium, Germany, Egypt, India and Norway.

ABOVE: **US Navy unit HS-11 'The Dragonslayers' operated the SH-3 Sea King with distinction for a number of years, and played a significant role in astronaut recovery operations following NASA space flights.**

Westland (Sikorsky) Sea King HC.4

First flight: May 7, 1969 (prototype)
Power: Two Roll-Royce Gnome 1,660shp H.1400-1T turboshafts
Armament: Torpedoes and depth charges
Size: Rotor diameter – 18.9m/62ft
Length – 17.02m/55ft 10in
Height – 4.72m/15ft 6in
Weights: Empty – 5,620kg/12,390lb
Maximum take-off – 9,752kg/21,500lb
Performance: Maximum speed – 245kph/152mph
Service ceiling – 3,050m/10,000ft
Range – 1,230km/764 miles (unladen)
Climb – 619m/2,030ft per minute

LEFT: **The Wasp could be armed to the teeth with missiles, torpedoes or depth charges and provided the Royal Navy with the ability to increase the reach of the weapons available to it at the time. Although effective as a submarine killer, it had to be deployed with a Wessex submarine hunter. It was taken out of front-line service in the late 1970s when the more capable and deadly Lynx arrived.**

Westland Wasp

The Westland Wasp was a small, gas turbine powered, shipboard anti-submarine helicopter derived from the P.531 programme that began as a Saunders-Roe design before that company was absorbed by Westland. The same programme also produced the British Army's Westland Scout and at one point the naval aircraft was to be called the Sea Scout. The Wasp differed from the land-based Scout by having a characteristic four-wheeled (quadricycle) castering undercarriage (as opposed to skids) for easy manoeuvring on flight decks, increased fuel capacity for longer over-water operations and a folding tail unit and rotor blades for easy stowage in small hangars on frigates.

The Wasp is a classic Cold War design that met the Royal Navy's Manned Torpedo-Carrying Helicopter (MATCH) requirement for a helicopter small enough to land on the deck of a frigate but able to carry two homing torpedoes. MATCH came about because of the increasing speed and attack range of the Soviet submarine fleet and the increased range at which the enemy subs could be, and had to be, detected and neutralized. The Wasp was in effect a stand-off weapons system that gave the Royal Navy an anti-submarine reach beyond the range of the weapons it carried on board its warships of the time. However, as the Wasp had no sonar of its own, it had to take its instructions from its parent ship.

The prototype naval P.531 first flew on October 28, 1962, and production followed soon after with 98 Wasps being built for the Royal Navy. The type was in front-line use soon after from mid-1963. Later in its service the Wasp was modified to carry the SS.11 wire-guided missile to target small surface vessels

ABOVE: **Deck crew, wearing white to make themselves as visible as possible, and firefighters stand by as a Wasp prepares to start engines and leave the small flight deck of HMS *Nubian*. A Royal Navy Tribal-class frigate launched on September 6, 1960, *Nubian* entered the Reserve in 1979, and was sunk as a target in 1987. RIGHT: A Lynx HAS.1 of 829 NAS with HMS *Aurora* in the background. Note the size of the two torpedoes in comparison to the helicopter itself.**

LEFT: **Another shot featuring HMS *Nubian*, as a Wasp prepares to land. Note the simple iron-bedstead castering undercarriage which absorbed bumpy deck landings and allowed crews to manhandle and move the small but potent helicopter with comparative ease.** BELOW: **A Royal Navy Wasp armed with two examples of the wire-guided SS.11 missile. This required the fitting of an observer's sight in the cabin roof and the installation of inflatable emergency floats in sponsons on either side of the cabin to prevent capsizing of the top-heavy aircraft in the event of a ditching.**

so an observer's sight was installed in the cabin roof. Also large inflatable emergency floats were added on either side of the cabin to improve survival chances in the event of a ditching.

As the more capable Westland Lynx entered service in the late 1970s, the Wasp was gradually withdrawn from front-line use. That was until 1982 and the Falklands War when seven mothballed Royal Navy frigates and their helicopters were recommissioned for active service in the South Atlantic.

On April 25, 1982, the Argentine submarine *Santa Fe* was spotted and attacked by a Wessex from HMS *Antrim*. HMS *Plymouth* launched a Wasp HAS. Mk 1 and HMS *Brilliant* launched a Westland Lynx to join the attack. The Wasp from HMS *Plymouth* as well as two other Wasps launched from HMS *Endurance* fired AS.12 anti-ship missiles at the submarine, scoring hits that damaged the sub enough to prevent it from submerging thereby making it the first casualty of the sea war during the Falklands War. The Royal Navy Wasp was finally withdrawn from service in 1988 when the last of the frigates for which the helicopter had been designed was decommissioned.

The Wasp did, however, fly on elsewhere entering service with the Royal Malaysian Navy in May 1990, serving with that navy for a decade. The Royal New Zealand Navy acquired the first of its Wasps in 1966 and did not retire the type until 1998. The Wasp was also in service with Holland as well as the Brazilian, Indonesian and South African navies.

LEFT: **A number of mothballed Royal Navy ships and their Wasp helicopters were brought back into service for the Falklands War, thousands of miles from the UK. The Wasp was finally retired, this time for good, in 1988, some ten years after its first retirement.**

Westland Wasp HAS. Mk 1

First flight: October 28, 1962 (naval prototype)
Power: One Rolls-Royce 710shp Nimbus Mk 503 turboshaft
Armament: Torpedoes, depth charges or anti-ship missiles, dependent on mission
Size: Rotor diameter – 9.83m/32ft 3in
Length – 9.24m/30ft 4in
Height – 3.56m/11ft 8in
Weights: Empty – 1,565kg/3,452lb
Maximum take-off – 2,495kg/5,500lb
Performance: Maximum speed – 193kph/120mph
Service ceiling – 3,813m/12,500ft
Range – 488km/303 miles
Climb – 439m/1,440ft per minute

LEFT: **The Westland Wessex in its many forms served the British military well for over two decades as a rescue, transport (sometimes Royal), and as a submarine killer. The single-turbine jet pipe tells us this is a Gnome-powered machine.**

Westland Wessex

In 1955, only a year after the piston-engined Sikorsky S-58 first flew in the US, the Royal Navy had issued a requirement for a turbine-engined ASW helicopter. Westland's submission was a licence-built version of the Sikorsky design already destined for US Navy use but modified for turbine-power. The nose had to be redesigned to accommodate the larger British engine, which exhausted through a pair of bifurcated exhaust pipes port and starboard beneath the front of the cockpit.

The first all-Westland-built machine, by now named Wessex, flew at Yeovil in June 1958, and deliveries to the Royal Navy began in less than two years in April 1960. The helicopter entered RN squadron service with No.815 NAS at Culdrose in July 1961, and a total of 11 squadrons ultimately operated the HAS. Mk 1 version, the first purpose-designed ASW helicopter operated by the Fleet Air Arm. The only offensive weapons carried by this version were torpedoes. Crew included an observer and an underwater control operator who manned the dipping sonar that listened for enemy submarines. The helicopter's tail assembly folded back against the fuselage to save space onboard ship.

The Wessex was also ordered by the RAF as the HC. Mk 2 for use as a troop transport. Seventy-four were built and a number were later converted for SAR duties. These also differed from the HC.1 by having a different engine or rather engines – two Rolls-Royce Gnome engines coupled to a common drive. The HC. Mk 2 could carry 16 troops or 1,814kg/4,000lb slung beneath it with just half of its coupled powerplant operating. The Gnome-powered versions can be readily identified by having just one, bigger, exhaust pipe on each side. A similar version to the HC.2, the HU.5 was ordered for the Royal Marines, with the first being delivered in December 1963, only six months after the prototype first flew. Among the differences was the addition of rapid-inflation flotation bags stowed in drums that extended outwards from the wheel hubs of the main undercarriage legs. These would have been 'fired' in the event of an emergency water landing. Six squadrons operated the HU.5 until 1987 having used the mark in action in Borneo and the Falklands.

Better radar equipment (including a large dorsal radome for a search radar), more engine power and the ability to carry

LEFT: **This SAR Wessex has its flotation bags deployed. Normally stowed in hub-mounted drums on the helicopter's main wheels, the bags would rapidly inflate when required, thanks to a cylinder of high-pressure gas carried on the inside of each wheel assembly.** ABOVE: **Retrieved from the carrier's hangar, this Wessex is being 'unfolded' and readied for flight.**

LEFT: **A Wessex HAS. Mk 3 prepares for take-off. The two exhaust pipes tell us this is a Gazelle-powered example. Note the winch/hoist assembly and the safety covers over the flotation bag stowage drums.**
BELOW: **The Wessex HU.5 was an important asset for the Royal Marines who used 100 examples of the tough and reliable helicopter for troop moving and supply as shown here. These machines went wherever the Royal Marines were deployed and so saw plenty of action.**

torpedoes, depth charges and wire-guided missiles were features of the HAS.3, which entered FAA service in January 1967. The radome's position led, inevitably, to this version being called the 'Camel'. Apart from three development aircraft, all HAS.3s were converted or, more accurately, rebuilt HAS.1s and remained in squadron service until December 1982 having had a reprieve for use in the Falklands War earlier that year.

XP142, an HAS. Mk 3 was operating from the Royal Navy destroyer HMS *Antrim* when it reached the South Atlantic before the main British task force in April 1982. On April 22 it rescued an SAS reconnaissance party from a glacier after their own Wessex HU.5s had crashed in a blizzard. On April 25, flown by Lt Cmdr I. Stanley, XP142 attacked, depth charged and helped to disable the Argentine submarine *Santa Fe*. Although the helicopter was subsequently damaged by enemy small-arms fire and bomb splinters, his historic aircraft is now preserved by the Fleet Air Arm Museum at Yeovilton in the UK.

ABOVE: **The tell-tale hump to the rear of the rotor assembly identifies this as a Wessex HAS. Mk 3. The 'hump' was a dorsal radome that housed a rotating search radar scanner that could pinpoint enemy submarines. Inevitably nicknamed 'the camel', this mark of Royal Navy Wessex saw much action in the Falklands War, the most famous being XP142 that attacked an Argentine submarine.**

Westland Wessex HAS. Mk 3

First flight: May 17, 1958 (Westland-rebuilt S-58)
Power: One Napier Gazelle 1,600shp 165 free power turbine
Armament: Torpedoes and depth charges
Size: Rotor diameter – 17.07m/56ft
Length – 20.07m/65ft 10in
Height – 4.85m/15ft 11in
Weights: Empty – 3,583kg/7,900lb
Maximum take-off – 6,168kg/13,600lb
Performance: Maximum speed – 212kph/132mph
Service ceiling – 3,050m/10,000ft
Range – 628km/390 miles
Climb – 503m/1,650ft per minute

LEFT: **XK906 was a Whirlwind HAS.7, the first ever type of British helicopter designed specifically for the anti-submarine role. Of the 129 supplied to the Royal Navy, the Royal Marines took delivery of 12 examples for communications/transport use.**
BELOW: **A Royal Navy Whirlwind gives a demonstration of Search-And-Rescue (SAR) on the deck of a British aircraft carrier. The Whirlwind was a reassuring presence for Fleet Air Arm aircrew as it hovered nearby during take-offs and landings.**

Westland (Sikorsky) Whirlwind

As helicopter design and technology improved after World War II, so the appreciation of the military applications of rotary craft grew. By the early 1950s, helicopters began to be used by the military in greater numbers but Britain's domestic helicopter industry was small and not at the cutting edge of design. Instead, the best way for Britain to quickly acquire a domestically produced helicopter fleet was by building American-designed helicopters under licence. So it was that Westland Helicopters of Yeovil built the Sikorsky S-55 helicopter in the mid-1950s as the Whirlwind. Westland made a number of improvements to the design over the years and the Whirlwind went on to serve in large numbers with the British Army, Royal Navy and Royal Air Force.

Britain's first Whirlwinds were in fact Sikorsky-built models acquired for evaluation. Ten examples of the HAS. Mk 21 rescue versions and twelve HAS. Mk 22 anti-submarine warfare machines were

successfully trialled in the UK leading to a licensing agreement. The first British Whirlwind HAR.1 flew on August 15, 1953 powered by the 600shp Pratt & Whitney Wasp. Serving in non-combat SAR roles, it was followed into service by the HAR.3 with a more powerful 700hp Wright R-1300-3 Cyclone 7 engine. It was 1955 before the HAR.5 flew for the first time with a British engine, the Alvis Leonides Major.

The only dedicated anti-submarine Whirlwind, the more advanced HAS.7, first flew on October 17, 1956, and entered Royal Navy squadron service with 845 NAS. in August 1957. This version was equipped with radar and dipping ASDIC for detecting submarines and could carry a torpedo, but could not carry both at the same time. Nevertheless, this aircraft pioneered rotary wing anti-submarine warfare capability for the Royal Navy.

Fleet Air Arm units operating the Whirlwind included Nos.814, 815,

820, 824, 845, 847 and 848 Naval Air Squadrons as well as Nos.705 and 771 Training Squadrons. Surplus HAS.7s were converted for use in the SAR role from 1960 becoming HAR.9s. The HAR.1, HAR.3 and HA.R5 were retired from service by the mid-1960s but the HAS.7 continued in use as a training helicopter until 1975.

LEFT: **The nose of the Westland Whirlwind contained the engines – note the line of engine-cooling air-intake grilles running beneath the helicopter's windscreen. The Whirlwind flew on in Royal Navy service until 1975.**

Westland (Sikorsky) Whirlwind HAR.3 SAR

First flight: August 15, 1953 (HAR.1)
Power: One Wright 700hp 165 R-1300-3 Cyclone 7
Armament: None
Size: Rotor diameter – 16.15m/53ft
Length – 12.88m/42ft 3in
Height – 4.06m/13ft 4in
Weights: Empty – 2,381kg/5,250lb
Maximum take-off – 3,583kg/7,900lb
Performance: Maximum speed – 180kph/112mph
Service ceiling – 4,815m/15,800ft
Range – 579km/360 miles
Climb – 336m/1,100ft per minute

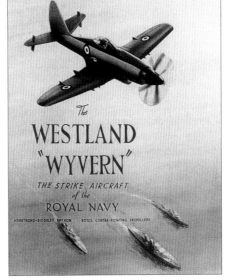

Westland Wyvern

The Westland Wyvern was another British aircraft that began its life with the unfortunate designation 'torpedo-fighter'. Despite the lessons learned during World War II and with aircraft like the Firebrand, some still thought that the two roles of daylight fighter and torpedo-bomber could sit together in one effective aircraft.

And so the Wyvern was proposed in response to specification N.11/44, issued in November 1944, calling for a single-seat ship-based strike fighter powered by a Rolls-Royce Eagle piston engine, but with the flexibility to accept a turboprop. The aircraft had to be carrier-capable, armed with four 20mm cannon, eight rockets, bombs, a mine or a torpedo. The RAF too had considered the same aircraft as a land-based fighter, but the lure of jet fighters proved too great.

Westland's aircraft had a half-elliptical wing similar to that of the Tempest but with an inverted gentle gull-wing configuration that folded for carrier operations. The first flight was made on December 12, 1946, followed by five further prototypes and ten pre-production aircraft. The aircraft were dogged with problems, most of which centred on the Eagle engine which was soon discarded to be replaced by a turboprop. The turboprop route was far from plain sailing and it was not until March 1949 that the first Armstrong Siddeley Python-engined Wyvern TF.2 took to the air.

Carrier trials began on June 21, 1950, and the Wyvern finally entered Fleet Air Arm service with 813 Sqadron in May 1953, replacing the Blackburn Firebrand. The standard service model was the Wyvern S. Mk 4. In November 1956, Nos.830 and 831 Squadrons took part in the Suez campaign, losing 2 aircraft in 79 sorties. No.813, the last front-line Wyvern unit was disbanded in March 1958. The

ABOVE LEFT: **This picture of a Wyvern on the catapult waiting for launch shows many of this aircraft's key features. Note the distinctive cockpit canopy shape and the pilot's field of vision, the large tail, the additional small fin on the tailplane and the turboprop exhaust pipe above the starboard wing fillet. The Wyvern was fitted with a Martin Baker ejector seat which saved the lives of many FAA pilots including one who ejected from underwater when his aircraft went into the sea after a failed catapult launch.** ABOVE: **A contemporary magazine advertisement billing the Wyvern as 'the' strike aircraft of the Royal Navy.**

Wyvern was a powerful, promising and groundbreaking aircraft that packed a punch but its delayed entry into service meant the type lost momentum that was never regained. Total Wyvern production reached 127 and it was the last fixed-wing military type produced by Westland.

ABOVE: **During the type's Suez combat use, one Wyvern was hit by Egyptian anti-aircraft fire and glided for three miles out to sea before the pilot ejected near the carrier HMS** *Eagle*. **The other was lost due to an exploding engine. The Wyvern's combat history is often overlooked.**

Westland Wyvern S.4

First flight: December 12, 1946

Power: One Armstrong Siddeley 4,110ehp 101 turboprop

Armament: Four 20mm cannon, sixteen 27kg/60lb rockets and 907kg/2,000lb of bombs, mines, depth charges or torpedoes

Size: Wingspan – 13.41m/44ft
Length – 12.88m/42ft 3in
Height – 4.8m/15ft 9in
Wing area – 32.98m²/355sq ft

Weights: Empty – 7,080kg/15,608lb
Maximum take-off – 11,115kg/24,500lb

Performance: Maximum speed – 632kph/393mph
Service ceiling – 8,535m/28,000ft
Range – 1,450km/900 miles
Climb – 2,135m/7,000ft per minute

LEFT: **The Yak-38 was the world's second operational V/STOL combat aircraft, but its career was comparatively short, while the Harrier that inspired it flourished.** BELOW: **It was not until 1978 that the Yak-38 entered service.**

Yakovlev Yak-38

Based on the experimental Yak-36M V/STOL research aircraft, Yakovlev developed the Yak-38 which became the first Soviet combat aircraft designed purely for carrier operation to enter series production. The Yak-38 was also the first production vertical take-off/landing aircraft built by the Soviet Union. Though inspired by the British Harrier, the Yak-38 had a completely different configuration to the British jump-jet. While the Harrier had one versatile engine, the Yak-38 had an engine in the rear used for forward flight while two other smaller, less powerful engines housed just aft of the cockpit were used purely for vertical take-off and landing. This added greatly to the aircraft's weight and reduced its fuel capacity.

Designed to perform fleet air defence, reconnaissance and anti-shipping strikes, the first flight of the Yak-36M prototype in conventional mode took place on January 15, 1971. Sea trials are known to have taken place in 1972 aboard the *Moskva* cruiser. A series of pre-production aircraft equipped an evaluation unit that operated from the 'carrier' *Kiev* in the summer of 1976 when the West got its first close look at the type as the *Kiev* entered the Mediterranean via the Bosporus. Six aircraft sat on the deck of the *Kiev* although only three were operational. By the end of the cruise, only one remained serviceable.

It was later in that year that the improved version, the Yak-38, entered production. The Yak-38, codenamed 'Forger' by NATO due to its Harrier inspiration, entered Soviet Navy service in 1978, based on four Kiev-class aircraft carriers, and two years later saw some action in Afghanistan.

LEFT: **The improved Yak-38M first flew in 1982 and featured the new, more powerful Tumansky R-28-300 vectored-thrust engine and the Kolesov RD-38 lift jet, each of which offered around 10 per cent greater thrust than the earlier engines. Despite these improvements, the aircraft remained in service for only a short time.**

LEFT: **When the Yak-36M appeared, it aroused great interest in the West until analysts realized that the basic design suffered from performance limitations.** ABOVE: **NATO aircraft took photos of the Yakovlev type whenever possible, so that the West could assess the threat the aircraft might pose. The Yak-38's shocking performance in high temperature says it all.**

The Yak-38's poor performance greatly limited its usefulness. In high temperatures the aircraft reportedly had an endurance of just 15 minutes and could carry only a small payload. The four Yak-38s deployed to Afghanistan in 1980 were operating in 'hot and high' conditions that highlighted the type's shortcomings. A total of 12 combat sorties were flown but the struggling aircraft could only carry two 100kg/220lb bombs each. Even with a greatly reduced fuel and weapons load, the Yak-38 proved incapable of operating during the hot daylight hours so its operations were restricted to pre 05:00 hours. In early hot-weather trials the lift jets refused to start at all and this was remedied by the installation of an oxygen-boosting intake system that was then fitted as standard.

The aircraft was not popular with pilots because of its poor performance and worse safety record. The lift engines had a life of around 22 hours and if one failed (always at low level), the aircraft then experienced a terrifying unrecoverable roll. To protect the pilot in this eventuality (a third of the Yak-38 fleet were lost in accidents), an automatic system ejected the pilot if it detected an engine failure. A more positive automated system was the Yak-38's hands-free landing capability. On approach, the aircraft could acquire a telemetry link from a computer system on the aircraft carrier which would then guide the aircraft on to the deck while the pilot just monitored the systems. Western observers were unsure of the aircraft's ability to make rolling take-offs but successful trials were carried out in December 1979.

Some 231 Yak-38 aircraft were produced in all, including 38 two-seat trainers (the Yak-38U). The Forger was withdrawn from front-line service in 1992–93, although a few remained in the inventory during 1994 as training aircraft.

This aircraft could not be described as a classic but rather a clear demonstration of the Soviet Union's need to be seen to be able to develop and utilize the same technological developments as the West – the Tupolev Tu-144 'Concordski' being another similar example. Seen as a stopgap aircraft while Soviet V/STOL technology was perfected, the next-generation aircraft never came.

ABOVE: **The hinged door that can be seen behind the cockpit was the air intake for the aircraft's lift jets. The 'Forger' was basic, had no radar warning system, and never posed a real threat to NATO.**

Yakovlev Yak-38

First flight: January 15, 1971 (Yak-36M)
Power: One Tumansky 6,813kg/15,020lb thrust R-28 V-300 turbofan and two Rybinsk 3,575kg/7,882lb thrust RD-38 turbofans for lift
Armament: Two gun pods and up to 500kg/1,100lb of bombs or missiles
Size: Wingspan – 7.32m/24ft
Length – 15.5m/50ft 10in
Height – 4.4m/14ft 4in
Wing area – 18.5m^2/199sq ft
Weights: Empty – 7,485kg/16,500lb
Maximum take-off – 11,700kg/25,795lb
Performance: Maximum speed – 1,050kph/655mph
Service ceiling – 12,000m/39,370ft
Range – 500km/310 miles
Climb – 4,500m/14,765ft per minute

Glossary

AAM Air-to-Air Missile.

aerodynamics Study of how gases, including air, flow and how forces act upon objects moving through air.

AEW Airborne Early Warning.

afterburner Facility for providing augmented thrust by burning additional fuel in the jet pipe.

ailerons Control surfaces at trailing edge of each wing used to make the aircraft roll.

AMRAAM Advanced Medium-Range Air-to-Air Missile.

angle of attack Angle of a wing to the oncoming airflow.

ASRAAM Advanced Short-Range Air-to-Air Missile.

ASV Air-to-Surface-Vessel – pertaining to this type of radar developed during World War II.

ASW Anti-Submarine Warfare.

AWACS Airborne Warning and Control System.

blister A streamlined, often clear, large fairing on aircraft body housing guns or electronics.

BVR Beyond Visual Range.

canard wings Two small horizontal surfaces on either side of the front of an aircraft.

CAP Combat Air Patrol.

ceiling The maximum height at which an aircraft can operate.

delta wing A swept-back, triangular-shaped wing.

dihedral The upward angle of the wing formed where the wings connect to the fuselage.

dorsal Pertaining to the upper side of an aircraft.

drag The force that resists the motion of the aircraft through the air.

ECM Electronic Counter Measures.

elevators Control surfaces on the horizontal part of the tail that are used to alter the aircraft's pitch.

ELINT Electronic Intelligence.

eshp Equivalent shaft horsepower.

FAA Fleet Air Arm.

FBW Fly-By-Wire.

fin The vertical portion of the tail.

flaps Moveable parts of the trailing edge of a wing used to increase lift at slower air speeds.

g The force of gravity.

HOTAS Hands-On Throttle And Stick.

hp Horsepower.

HUD Head-Up Display.

IFF Identification Friend or Foe.

jet engine An engine that works by creating a high-velocity jet of air to propel the engine forward.

JMSDF Japanese Maritime Self-Defense Force.

leading edge The front edge of a wing or tailplane.

Mach Speed of sound – Mach 1 = 1,223kph/706mph at sea level.

monoplane An aircraft with one set of wings.

NATO North Atlantic Treaty Organization.

pitch Rotational motion in which an aircraft turns around its lateral axis.

port Left side.

RAAF Royal Australian Air Force.

radome Protective covering for radar made from material through which radar beams can pass.

RAF Royal Air Force.

RATO Rocket-Assisted Take-Off.

RCAF Royal Canadian Air Force.

reheat *See* afterburner.

RFC Royal Flying Corps.

RN Royal Navy.

roll Rotational motion in which the aircraft turns around its longitudinal axis.

rudder The parts of the tail surfaces that control an aircraft's yaw (its left and right turning).

SAM Surface-to-Air Missile.

SLR Side-Looking airborne Radar.

starboard Right side.

STOL Short Take-Off and Landing.

supersonic Indicating motion faster than the speed of sound.

swing wing A wing capable of variable sweep e.g. on Panavia Tornado.

tailplane Horizontal part of the tail, known as horizontal stabilizer in North America.

thrust Force produced by engine which pushes an aircraft forward.

triplane An aircraft with three sets of wings.

UHF Ultra High Frequency.

USAAF United States Army Air Forces.

USAF United States Air Force.

USCG United States Coast Guard.

USMC United States Marine Corps.

USN United States Navy.

V/STOL Vertical/Short Take-Off and Landing.

variable geometry *See* swing wing.

ventral Pertaining to the underside of an aircraft.

VHF Very High Frequency.

Key to flags

For the specification boxes, the national flag that was current at the time of the aircraft's use is shown.

 France

 Italy

 Japan

 UK

 USA

 USSR

Index

A

Afghanistan, 124
Agusta Westland Merlin,
    7, 30–1
aircraft carriers
    21st century, 22–3
    countries maintaining, 24
    current and future, 24–5
    and Libya, 20–1, 64, 71
    Nimitz-class, 24, 25
    see also warships
aircraft weapons
    cannon
        30mm GIAT/DEFA, 14
        M61A1 20mm Gatling
            Gun, 23
        Mauser MG-213, 14
    missiles
        AGM Maverick, 14
        AIM-9 Sidewinder, 12, 14
        AIM-120, 14
        categories of, 14–15
        Phoenix, 15
    see also individual aircraft
        entries
Albatross, Beriev A-40/
    Be-42, 36–7
Alizé, Breguet, 46–7
Alvarez, Lt Everett Jr, 12
Armstrong Whitworth (Hawker),
    Sea Hawk, 6, 32–3
Attacker, Supermarine, 108

B

BAE SYSTEMS
    Harrier, 7, 16, 19, 34–5
    Sea Harrier, 7, 16, 17, 19,
        24–5
Balkans, 71, 117
Banshee, McDonnell F2H, 87
Be-12, Beriev, 38–9
Beriev
    A-40/Be-42 Albatross, 36–7
    Be-12, 38–9
Blackburn Buccaneer, 40–1
Boeing B29 Superfortress, 11
Boeing/McDonnell Douglas/
    Northrop, FA-18
    Hornet/Super Hornet,
        21, 23, 42–5
Borneo, 120
Breguet, Alizé, 46–7
Buccaneer, Blackburn, 40–1

C

Carmichael, Lt Peter, 11, 78
Clinton, President Bill, 9

Corsair II, Vought A-7, 13,
    20, 21, 110–11
Corsair, Vought F4U, 10, 11
Cougar, Grumman F9F, 68–9
Crusader, Vought F-8, 112–13

D

Dassault
    Etendard and Super
        Etendard, 48–9
    Rafale, 8–9, 50–1
de Havilland
    Sea Venom, 6, 52–3
    Sea Vixen, 54–5
Demon, McDonnell F3H, 87
Douglas
    A-3 Skywarrior, 60–1
    FD4 Skyray, 58–9
    Skyraider, 10, 11, 13,
        56–7
Dragonfly, Westland, 100–1

E

Ely, Eugene B., 6
Etendard and Super Etendard,
    Dassault, 48–9

F

F-27, Fokker, 20
F-35, Lockheed Martin, 7
F-111, General Dynamics, 20, 21
Fairey Gannet, 62–3
Falklands War, 16–17, 89,
    117, 118, 120, 121
Firefly, Fairey, 10, 11
Fokker, F-27, 20
Fury, North American FJ, 94–5

G

Gannet, Fairey, 62–3
General Dynamics, F-111,
    20, 21
Grumman
    A-6 Intruder, 21, 64–5
    EA-6B Prowler, 20, 21
    F7F Tigercat, 74
    F9F Cougar, 68–9
    F9F Panther, 10, 11, 66–7
    F11F Tiger, 72–3
    F-14 Tomcat, 15, 20, 26,
        27, 29, 70–1
    Tracker, 75
Grumman/Northrop
    Grumman, E-2
    Hawkeye, 76–7
Gulf War, 64, 71, 80, 90,
    110, 115, 117

H

Harrier, BAE SYSTEMS,
    7, 16, 19, 34–5
Hawker Sea Fury, 10, 78–8
Hawkeye, Grumman/
    Northrop Grumman E-2,
        76–7
Hornet/Super Hornet,
    Boeing/McDonnell
    Douglas/Northrop
    FA-18, 21, 23, 42–5

I

Intruder, Grumman A-6, 21, 64–5

J

jet engine technology, 18
Johnson, President Lyndon, 12

K

Ka-25, Kamov, 81
Ka-27, Kamov, 81
Kaman, SH-2 Seasprite, 80
Kamov
    Ka-25, 81
    Ka-27, 81
Korean War, 10–11, 56, 66,
    67, 74, 78, 87

L

Libya, 20–1
Lightning II, Lockheed
    Martin F-35, 84–5
Lippisch, Alexander, 58
Lockheed S-3 Viking, 82–3
Lockheed Martin F-35
    Lightning II, 84–5
Lynx, Westland, 114–15

M

McDonnell
    F2H Banshee, 87
    F3H Demon, 87
McDonnell Douglas
    A-4 Skyhawk, 13, 26, 88–9
    F-4 Phantom II, 90–1

F4 Phantom, 12, 26
Marlin, Martin P5M, 86
Martin P5M Marlin, 86
Merlin, Agusta Westland, 7, 30–1
Mikoyan-Gurevitch
    MiG-15, 10, 11
    MiG-17, 13, 14, 26
    MiG-21, 26
    MiG-23, 21, 71
    MiG-25, 20, 21
    MiG-29K, 92–3
Mirror Landing Aid (MLA), 19
missiles, aircraft weapons, 12, 14

N

naval aircraft
    bent-wing, 9
    compared to land types, 6
    flying boats, 7
    helicopters, 7
    technology 1945 to
        present, 18–19
naval aircraft armament
    see aircraft weapons
North American
    A3J/A5 Vigilante, 12, 96–7
    FJ Fury, 94–5
Northrop T-38 Talon, 26

P

Panther, Grumman F9F, 10,
    11, 66–7
Phantom, McDonnell
    Douglas F4, 12, 26
Phantom II, McDonnell
    Douglas F4, 90–1
Prowler, Grumman Ea-6B, 20, 21
PS-1/US-1, ShinMaywa, 98–9

R

Rafale, Dassault, 8–9, 50–1

S

S51, Sikorsky, 100–1
Scimitar, Supermarine, 15, 109
Sea Fury, Hawker, 10, 78–9

ABOVE: **Grumman F-14 Tomcat.**

ABOVE: **Agusta Westland EH 101 Merlin.**

Sea Harrier, BAE SYSTEMS,
7, 16, 17, 34–5
Sea Hawk, Armstrong Whitworth
(Hawker), 6, 32–3
Sea King, Westland (Sikorsky),
16, 116–17
Sea Stallion, Sikorsky CH-53E
and MH-53, 104–5
Sea Venom, de Havilland, 6,
52–3
Sea Vixen, de Havilland, 54–5
Seafire, Supermarine, 10
Seahawk, Sikorsky SH-60,
102–3
Seasprite, Kaman SH-2, 80
ShinMaywa, PS-1/US-1, 98–9
ships see warships
Sikorsky
CH-53E Sea Stallion and
MH-53, 104–5
S-51, 100–1
SH-60 Seahawk, 102–3
Skyhawk, McDonnell
Douglas A4, 13, 26, 88
Skyraider, Douglas, 10, 11,
12, 13, 56–7
Skyray, Douglas FD4, 58–9
Skywarrior, Douglas A-3, 60–1
Su-22, Sukhoi, 21
Su-33, Sukhoi, 106–7
Sukhoi Su-33, 106–7
Superfortress, Boeing B29,
11
Supermarine
Attacker, 108
Scimitar, 15, 109
Seafire, 10

T
Talon, Northrop T-38, 26
Tiger, Grumman F11F, 72–3
Tigercat, Grumman F7F, 74
Tomcat, Grumman F-14, 15,
20, 26, 27, 29, 70–1
Top Gun, 13, 26–7
Tracker, Grumman, 75

U
United States Navy Fighter
Weapons School
(Top Gun), 13, 26–7

V
Vietnam War, 12–13, 60,
64, 86, 90, 91, 110, 113
Vigilante, North American
A3J/A5, 12, 96–7
Viking, Lockheed S-3, 82–3
Vought
A-7 Corsair II, 13, 20, 21,
110–11
F-8 Crusader, 112–13
F4U Corsair, 10, 11

W
warships
Argentina
Santa Fe, 115, 119, 121
France
Charles de Gaulle, 25, 51, 76
Clemenceau, 113
Foch, 51, 113
India (INS), Vikramaditya, 92
Royal Australian Navy
(HMAS), Sydney, 11, 78
Royal Navy (HMS)
Albion, 32, 53
Antrim, 119, 121
Ark Royal (No. 4), 34,
40, 41, 54
Ark Royal (No. 5), 117
Birmingham, 114
see also United States
vessel
Bulwark, 18, 32
Centaur, 54
Coventry, 89, 115
Eagle, 32, 53
Endurance, 119
Glasgow, 89, 115
Glory, 11, 78
Hermes (Falklands),
16–17

Illustrious, 16, 62
Nubian, 118
Ocean, 11, 78, 116
Plymouth, 119
Prince of Wales
(planned), 25
Queen Elizabeth
(planned), 25
SS Atlantic Conveyer
(carrier conversion), 16
Theseus, 11, 78
Triumph, 10
Victorious, 54, 109
Russia, Admiral
Kuznetsov, 25
United States (USS)
Abraham Lincoln, 24, 44
America, 20, 76
Antietam, 32
Badoing Strait, 10
see also Royal Navy
vessel
Bon Homme Richard, 67, 72
Boxer, 10, 66, 94
Constellation, 12, 83
Coral Sea, 20, 21
Enterprise (1960s/Vietnam),
13, 97
Enterprise (Current), 22,
23, 25, 76
Forrestal, 13, 60, 72
Intrepid, 72
Maddox, 12, 113
Nicholas, 22
Nimitz, 24, 25, 71
Oriskany, 13
Pennsylvania, 9
Philippine Sea, 10
Princeton, 11
Ranger, 72
Saratoga, 20, 72, 96
Theodore Roosevelt, 71
Ticonderoga, 12, 113
Valley Forge, 10, 66
Wasp, Westland, 15, 118–19
Wessex, Westland, 18, 120–1
Westland
Dragonfly, 100–1
Lynx, 114–15
Wasp, 15, 118–19
Wessex, 18, 120–21
Wyvern, 19, 123
Westland (Sikorsky) Sea King,
16, 116–17
Whirlwind, 122
Whirlwind, Westland (Sikorsky),
122
Wyvern, Westland, 19, 123

Y
Yakovlev, Yak-38, 19, 124–5

Acknowledgements

The publisher would like to thank
the following individuals and picture
libraries for the use of their pictures in
the book. Every effort has been made
to acknowledge the pictures properly,
however we apologize if there are any
unintentional omissions, which will
be corrected in future editions.

l=left, r=right, t=top, b=bottom,
m=middle, um = upper middle,
lm= lower middle

Michael J.F. Bowyer: 15b, 34tr, 48t,
48bl, 49b, 55m, 55b, 58b, 112b, 113tr.
Francis Crosby Collection: 6t, 17bl,
17br, 32t, 32b, 33tr, 33m, 35tl, 35tr,
41m, 41b, 52br, 54m, 54b, 55t, 57b,
58tr, 66b, 69b, 74tr, 89b, 91tr, 100br,
108t, 108b, 109tl, 109tr, 113tl, 114b,
116tr, 117m, 120bl, 120br, 121t, 121m,
121b, 122t, 122m, 122b, 123tr.
Chris Farmer: 40tl, 54t, 56t, 57t, 65b,
75t, 78t, 78b, 83t, 110m, 111m, 112t.
Felicity Forster: 102b.
Brian Marsh: 33tl.
Geoff Sheward: 40tr, 61tr, 65tr, 75t,
76tr, 80tr, 82t, 83t, 88t, 88b, 89t, 89m,
110t, 111t, 111b, 117b, 120t.
TRH Pictures: 1, 2, 3, 5, 6b, 7t, 7bl,
7br, 8–9, 10t, 10b, 11tl, 11tr, 11m, 11b,
12t, 12b,13tl, 13tr, 13b, 14t, 14b, 15tl,
15tr, 15m, 16t, 16b, 17tl, 17tr, 17mr,
18t, 18b, 19tl, 19tr, 19mr, 19b, 20t, 20b,
21tl, 21tr, 21bl, 21br, 23b, 24t, 24b,
25tl, 25tr, 25m, 25b, 26t, 26b, 27tl, 27tr,
27m, 27b, 28–9, 30t, 30b, 31tl, 31tr,
31m, 31b, 34tl, 35b, 36t, 36m, 36b,
37t, 38t, 38bl, 38br, 39t, 39m, 39b,
40b, 41t, 42tl, 42tr, 42b, 43tl, 43tr, 43b,
44t, 44b, 45t, 45ml, 45mr, 45b, 46tl,
46tr, 46b, 47t, 47m, 47b, 49t, 49m,
50tl, 50tr, 50b, 51t, 52t, 52bl, 53tl, 53tr,
53b, 58tl, 59t, 59m, 59b, 60t, 60b, 61tl,
61b, 62t, 62b, 63t, 63m, 63b, 64t, 65tl,
66t, 67t, 67um, 67lm, 67b, 68b, 69t,
69m, 70t, 70b, 71tl, 71tr, 71b, 72t, 72b,
73tl, 73tr, 73b, 74b, 76tl, 76b, 77tl, 77tr,
77b, 79t, 80tl, 80b, 81t, 81b, 84tl, 84tr,
84b, 85t, 85m, 85b, 86t, 86b, 87t, 87b,
90t, 90m, 90b, 91tl, 91b, 92tl, 92tr,
92bl, 92br, 93t, 93m, 93b, 94tl, 94tr,
94b, 95t, 95m, 95b, 96tl, 96tr, 96bl,
96br, 97t, 97b, 98t, 98b, 99tl, 99tr, 99b,
100t, 100bl, 101t, 101m, 101b, 102tl,
102tr, 103tl, 103tr, 103b, 104tl, 104b,
105t, 105m, 105b, 106t, 106bl, 106br,
107t, 107b, 109b, 110b, 113b, 118t,
118bl, 118br, 119t, 119m, 119b, 123tl,
123b, 124tl, 124tr, 124b, 125tl, 125tr,
125b, 127, 128, endpapers.
US Navy: 22t, 22b, 23tl, 23tr.
Nick Waller: 33b, 34b, 37m, 37b, 48br,
51b, 56b, 57m, 64b, 68t, 74tl, 79m,
79b, 82b, 104tr, 114tl, 114tr, 115t,
115m, 115b, 116tl, 116b, 117t.